That's Outside My Boat

BOAT ENTHUSIASTS

"*That's Outside My Boat* should be read by everyone who wants to add value to his or her life, relationships, and career. It teaches one of life's most valuable lessons in achieving success, both personally and professionally. Champions focus their energies on the things they can control. Everyone who reads it will come away re-energized with the tools he or she needs to take the checkered flag and become a champion."

JOE HEITZLER
Chairman of the Board, president, and CEO,
Championship Auto Racing Teams

"*That's Outside My Boat* is a marvelous guide to life—business and personal. Good lessons in each of fifty-five chapters."

—ROBERT MONDAVI
Chairman emeritus,
Robert Mondavi Family Wine

"*That's Outside My Boat* speaks very loudly to me, because that's the precise mentality that, when adopted, helped Acxiom focus solely on our core competencies and cast off those business ventures that weren't in our area of expertise. Our 'outside my boat' realization was directly responsible for the huge growth we've experienced in the last fifteen years. The lessons of personal experience expressed in this book will help anyone and everyone focus on what's really important in business and in life."

—CHARLES MORGAN
President and CEO, Acxiom Corporation

"In the political arena you are frequently faced with circumstances over which you have little or no control. *That's Outside My Boat* gives us the understanding and knowledge to face these challenges. It is a must-read for all aspiring leaders."

—DAVE COX
Assembly Republican Leader, California Assembly

"*That's Outside My Boat* is a perfect mix of real-life experiences presented in just the right size doses to keep your own life focused and stress-free."

"A personal strategy to control only what you can and let go of the rest is a simple concept yet a liberating one, because it reminds us of both our unique strengths and our personal limitations. *That's Outside My Boat* contains inspirational stories by those who have reached the pinnacle of success in their chosen fields and provides example after example of how this philosophy helped them overcome overwhelming challenges."

"In business, knowing what's 'in your boat' and what isn't is exactly the same thing as knowing how to listen to your customer or client. By listening you can be sure to provide the best and most beneficial goods and services to each of the people you do business with."

"These are great lessons that truly apply to all aspects of life, business, education, sports, and just plain everyday living."

—ROBERT A. YOUNG III
President and CEO, Arkansas Best Corporation

"Successful business people have learned from others and through trial and error. *That's Outside My Boat* offers unusually candid and dynamic stories of powerful life experiences that we can all learn from."

—ALEX G. SPANOS
Chairman of the board, A.G. Spanos Companies

"There is no question that *That's Outside My Boat* can help us accomplish more in our lives. It teaches us to not concern ourselves with those things over which we have no control, even wins and losses. Plus, this philosophy will make us a heck of a lot more enjoyable to be around."

—CHARLIE MONFORT
Vice chairman, Colorado Rockies

"Charlie and Kim have done it again. They have put together an informing and entertaining series of interviews from the world of business, academia, and sports. The sum of these interviews provide valuable lessons for business, family, and life."

—BOB WHALEN
President, Martin Marietta Orlando Aerospace

Books by
Kim Doren and Charlie Jones

You Go Girl!
Winning the Women's Way

Be The Ball
A Golf Instruction Book for the Mind

Game, Set, Match
A Tennis Book for the Mind

If Winning Were Easy, Everyone Would Do It
Motivational Quotes for Athletes

Heaven Can Wait
Surviving Cancer

You Go Girl!
A Journal to Get You There

Books by Charlie Jones

What Makes Winners Win
New York Times Bestseller

A Christmas to Remember

Christmas Memories of Mr. and Mrs. Santa Claus

That's Outside My Boat

•

LETTING GO OF WHAT YOU CAN'T CONTROL

Charlie Jones and Kim Doren

Charlie Jones is *The New York Times* best-selling author of *What Makes Winners Win*. A network sportscaster for four decades, he was inducted into the Pro Football Hall of Fame. Charlie holds a J.D. from the University of Arkansas Law School and lives in La Jolla, California.

Kim Doren has a diverse career that includes directing the marketing for Cobra Golf, teaching, media consulting, and working in Outback Australia as a jillaroo. A graduate of Stanford University, she loves sharing time with her nieces—Cassandra, Chloe, Alexa, Laura and Marie.

ISBN: 1-4392-0162-5
ISBN-13: 978-1-4392-0162-6

To my partner—WOW!

That goes for me, too.

Contents

Preface

Charlie

Two of the highlights of my thirty-three years as a sportscaster at NBC-TV were the 1988 Seoul Olympics and the 1992 Barcelona Olympics.

In Seoul, I covered all the excitement of track and field. This was Flo Jo's Games. She took home three gold medals and a silver medal. It was also the Olympics of Ben Johnson's world record of 9.79 seconds in the 100 meters that lasted only forty-eight hours before he was disqualified for steroids, all live, in prime time.

In Barcelona, it was the historic comeback of Pablo Morales in swimming, plus the diving venue featuring the most beautiful setting in Olympic history, with the entire city of Barcelona as the backdrop.

After this, naturally I was looking forward to my assignments at the 1996 Games in Atlanta. That is, until I received the phone call informing me I would be announcing rowing, canoeing, and kayaking.

Rowing, canoeing, and kayaking are watched only by rowers, canoers, kayakers, and their families, and they're on television at seven in the morning. The venue was Lake Lanier, an hour's drive outside Atlanta. I wouldn't even be at the Olympics.

Let's face it, when I arrived there a week before the Games I wasn't the happiest camper in the world, but then my broadcast partner, Bob Ernst, head crew coach at the University of Washington, and I started interviewing Olympic rowers from all over the world.

Not knowing the sport, I started with basic questions such as "What if it's raining?" The answer was "That's outside my boat." I asked, "What if the wind blows you off course?" Answer: "That's outside my boat." "What if you break an oar?" Same response: "That's outside my boat."

Finally I began to understand that these Olympic rowers were interested only in what they could control, to try to win an Olympic medal, and that was what was going on inside their boat. Then it slowly began to dawn on me that my assignment was "outside my boat." Dick Ebersol, then president of NBC Sports, hadn't called and asked me what I would like to cover; he had simply given me this venue. What I did with it was up to me.

Once I realized this, I was able to let the assignment go; it was "outside my boat." What was inside my boat, what I could control, was how Bob Ernst and I broadcast rowing.

From that point on, this became by far the best Olympics of my life. Bob and I had a great time together, from sharing doughnuts in the lobby of the Holiday Inn at 5 A.M. to our gourmet dinners across the street at Popeyes Famous Fried Chicken. From the friendly people of Gainesville, Georgia, without question the Hospitality Capital of the World, to broadcasting rowing, canoeing, and kayaking, truly pure Olympic sports.

I learned a great lesson from these Olympic rowers: let go of what you can't control, it really is "outside your boat." When I returned from the Atlanta Olympics, one of the first persons I shared this concept with was Kim Doren, my coauthor.

Kim

My first thought when Charlie told me his "That's outside my boat" experience was how much I needed to take this lesson to heart. I had just begun a planned yearlong sabbatical from corporate life and would soon be heading off to tour Europe and Central Asia. I was immediately reminded how much is outside my control when I'm traveling, particularly when my plans included a trek through Uzbekistan and Kyrgyzstan. Perhaps that's why I enjoy travel—it's always an unpredictable, exciting adventure and a constant challenge.

From my years in the golf industry I came up with the acronym "*par*" to remind me of what I *can* control: my *p*erformance, my *a*ttitude, and my *r*esponse. In other words, focus on what I can control—"*par*"—and stop worrying and wasting energy on things I have no power to control. It sounds so easy in the abstract. Of course, what is simple in theory is not necessarily simple in practice. In fact, I'm not sure I have a much better chance of shooting *"par"* in life than I do on a golf course!

Charlie and I realized that knowing *what* to do is definitely easier that knowing *how* to do it. *That's Outside My Boat* uses the power of the personal example to demonstrate the variety of ways business executives, scholars, artists, and athletes have succeeded by focusing on what they decide is important and letting go of what they can't control. Their various perspectives and experiences can help you discover how to apply "That's outside my boat" to your life and to your business. We hope that their stories will empower, inspire, and enlighten you. They certainly did that for us.

Introduction

BOB ERNST

University of Washington head crew coach and
former women's Olympic rowing coach

I N 1987, WE WERE REBUILDING the women's national
rowing team. We had won the Olympics in 1984, and
1985 was kind of a down year. In 1986, they asked me
to come back and be the coach again through the next
Olympics. We got the program underway and finished
fifth at the Worlds.

In 1987, the World Championships were held in
Copenhagen, Denmark. They have a racecourse that's one
of the worst two or three in the world. It's renowned for
its horrible winds. When you look at the course, lane one
is on the right-hand side and lane six is on the left-hand
side. The wind always blows from lane one toward lane
six. Lane one has a row of trees alongside it that is probably a hundred feet tall, so it's protected from the winds.
However, lane six is wide open and it's really windy.

We were in the finals, and the wind was blowing like
hell, and we were in lane six. There were twelve- to

eighteen-inch waves at the starting line. I mean, it was *Victory at Sea* out there. The event before ours was the women's quad, and the Dutch women were in lane six. As a statement of their displeasure at having to row in those kinds of conditions, they stopped in protest with 300 meters to go. They started yelling at the officials, and they even flipped off the television cameras.

I was thinking at that moment, Well, it's a rebuilding year, who knows what will happen to us. But actually I was really upset that we had to row in lane six. They started the race, and the kids were just amazing. I was watching it on TV from the finish line. They just went all out. It was rough all the way across the start, but it was rougher in lane six. They came down the track in lane six, right next to the television catamaran. I saw them on camera, and I yelled, "Holy cow! We're doing all right!" You could see the water flying over the kids' heads and the waves breaking on the bow girl's back. I said, "Oh, man, what's going on?"

Five hundred meters in, we were right there in first place. And I was thinking, No way. We had never beaten the Soviets at that point. They were a ten-megaton crew with an average height and weight of 6'1", 198 pounds. That was the *average*. And the East Germans were 6'1", 185 average. Our kids were midgets by international standards. We were 5'10", 168 average. Yet here we were coming down the racecourse. We got to 1,000 meters and the television cameras panned so you could see from one of the timing towers, and the Soviets weren't even in the picture.

I think the East Germans ended up fourth and the Soviets were fifth, and we were just edged out by the Romanians in the last 500 meters. But that was the best rowing inside our boat that I've ever seen, because it would have been so easy for those kids to have just dived overboard at the starting line. I have the videotape of the race, and when I look at it I think that if I'd been at the starting line, I'd have left town, because the waves were so high, it was so windy, and water was splashing in the boat. It was that rough.

Afterwards, the girls said they never gave the wind and the conditions a thought. All they were thinking about was Betsy, the coxswain, saying, "Okay, we're at a thousand meters and we've got three seats on the cows," referring to the Soviets. She was racing off of them the whole time. She said, "Okay, we're making history, let's go! Give me another ten. Let's take two more seats on 'em. It's nuclear war right here."

It's all about keeping focused on what you're doing and letting go of the things you can't control. That's what Charlie and Kim's book is all about, and when you do that you'll discover life really is great fun.

**THAT'S OUTSIDE
MY BOAT.**

Focus On What You Can Control

BOB WRIGHT

Chairman and CEO, NBC;
vice chairman and executive oficer, General Electric

I CAN'T WORK EFFECTIVELY until I get inside my boat. When I have unresolved personal problems that I'm struggling with, they come into my workday—they get inside my boat—and that makes it very difficult for me to perform. When I can successfully resolve them—separate them from my work—then work is a pleasure and is a lot easier to do. But if I'm worried about a bunch of things unrelated to my job, it's much harder for me to work. I start to get picky and everything becomes annoying.

I subscribe to the concept that no matter what you're doing, you're going to do it better and you're going to enjoy it more if you can, for a certain period of time, remove yourself from unrelated pressures and concerns. This is very important to me, because my personal life and my work life are highly interrelated. I can't really separate the two. I'm lucky to have a great family and a strong wife, Suzanne. We've been married for thirty-four years. She knows that I don't perform well if I'm grappling with problems concerning the kids or if I'm dealing with home issues, so she tries her best to cover them. If I carry these concerns to the office with me all day it's a real handicap. The ability to plan your life so you can focus on what's inside your boat is clearly the track for success and personal enjoyment.

However, there are some things you just can't resolve. What I try to do then is set up a plan to deal with those issues that makes me comfortable in knowing I'm doing the best I can. I put them outside my boat for a period. I say, "Okay, I've handled that for today." Then I feel I've earned the right not to have to worry about those issues right now, so I can work on what's inside my boat. The trick is organizing myself in such a way that I feel like I'm making enough progress so I can really focus on the task at hand, whatever it is—playing golf, giving a speech, or running a network. The problems arise when I can't convince myself that I have done the best I can. Then issues start to weigh on me, they encroach, they get inside my boat, and my performance drops off.

Sometimes when I come to work I feel like I'm a loser. I'm juggling six balls in the air and I'm not happy with any of them. That's tough on me and I know I'm not going to have a nice day. At those times I make it a point to convince myself early in the day that I'm doing a better job with some of those balls than I'm giving myself credit for. If I don't, they'll just hang over my head like big clouds. You can't be fighting battles all day against a series of things that are out of your control.

"Major successes are not built on success. They are built on failure, on frustration, sometimes even calamity, and how you deal with it, and how you turn it around from a negative to a positive."

—SUMNER REDSTONE
CEO, Viacom

"See life the way it is. Don't kid yourself."

—JACK WELCH
Chairman and CEO, General Electric

IT'S ONE THING TO SAY,
"THAT'S OUTSIDE
MY BOAT";
IT'S ANOTHER THING
TO BELIEVE IT.

Determine What Is Inside and What Is Outside Your Boat

DICK CAPEN
Former U.S. ambassador to Spain

WHEN I WAS PUBLISHER OF THE *MIAMI HERALD*, we had nine editions of the paper a day and a total of five major riots, each of which killed fifteen people. There were all kinds of controversy and death threats, and I often found myself the symbol of attack on many different fronts. The only way I could deal with it was to have a *Miami Herald* body and a Dick Capen body. Occasionally I'd put my soul, my personal life, and everything I really cared about off to the side to help me sustain the arrows of misfortune that would come my way. I think there are certain people who do that in their lives when they have a lot of responsibilities. They don't allow one aspect of their life to drag them down in a personal way.

If you have a specific set of values and priorities in your life and a sense of peace within yourself, you realize that the criticism is really aimed at the institution you represent or the responsibilities you have, rather than at you personally. There are times when people will attack everything you represent, your integrity and your reputation. That's when you go to general quarters, because those attacks are going right at your own persona.

However, we have a lot of different personas. We have a commentator persona, we have a family persona, and we have a group of friends with whom we relate, but I think you have to separate those. It takes a certain amount of discipline to do it. You need to not overreact when you are being criticized or when something's directed at you unfairly in a career sense or a competitive sense. You're not going to be an oarsman forever. It's a moment in your life and it's not going to drive your entire life.

I was just reading through some material on Hubert Humphrey, who talked a lot about his defeat in 1968, when he was running for president. He said that many people see a setback as a funeral of their life, rather than the beginning of another chapter. Instead of giving the invocation of a new beginning, they're giving the benediction of the end. They're not able to move on. "That's outside my boat" is another way of moving on.

"There's something deep and enduring within all of us that is so strong that unless we have been challenged we'd never have known we have it."

—MARTY HEAD
Businesswoman

"The pendulum will swing, and there will be another day. You just keep on keeping on, because you must."

—ANNE EVANS
Chairman, Evans Hotels

"Success is really just the management of failure."

—KAMRAN ELAHIAN
Cofounder, Cirrus Logic

3

Be Prepared with a Competitive Response

LIZ DOLAN

Former Nike corporate vice president
for global marketing, now president, Dolan St. Clair
Sports Marketing Consultants

W HEN I WAS WORKING AT NIKE, Reebok introduced
the shoe called "The Pump," which was a huge
deal in the industry for six months. It was billed as the
future of athletic shoes, and it gathered a tremendous
amount of outside attention from people who weren't
really in the athletic footwear business but who believed
this was where the business was heading. And even
though we did not believe this was the case because it
wasn't that functional or useful, we did have to respond
in some way. We could have said, "We're not doing
that." In that competitive environment, it would have
been the same as saying "That's outside my boat."

8

When a competitor makes a move, you can choose to ignore it or you can choose to respond to it. If you choose to respond to it, you can either do what they are doing better or do something else that gets the attention back on you.

Our response to "The Pump" was to try to build a shoe better than Reebok's. We developed our own product that we thought was more technically appropriate. It turned out to be a giant failure because this market condition change was very temporary. It was not a legitimate advance in the science of athletic shoes; it was a market gimmick. By chasing it we really wasted a fair amount of time and money.

Thinking back on that now, should we have ignored it? Should we have just said, "We don't believe in that, so we're not going to do it"? Maybe we should have. It was just a distraction. But we paid attention to it because it was distracting consumers, who seemed to like it. We felt we had to respond.

I think ego enters into it, ego in the best sense of wanting to be the market leader and believing that you should always be perceived as the market leader. It's a really important part of your brand identity. Nike was clearly the market and technology leader at the time, and so for another brand in our category to do something that appeared to give it a technical edge was not good.

Sometimes that ego stuff is bad. There are things you chase just because you want to be the coolest. We tried to avoid that and keep our eye on the ball of leadership. But if we saw something that made us feel as if a competitor was taking that position from us, and it was a serious threat to our brand identity, we reacted.

Phil Knight, Nike's CEO, has always said that the main thing he learned from Nike cofounder Bill Bowerman was *competitive response*, and as an athlete or as a businessperson you must be aware of what you have to do to respond to your competitors. An athlete is a winner not because he has more pure talent but because he knows what to do in a competitive environment when the person he's competing against does something. He has to respond. He has to respond at that very moment.

Phil Knight believed it was our job to run the business that way—not in a reactive way of watching what our competitors did and responding, but in always being willing to respond when somebody did something that was unexpected or that challenged us in an area where we felt we deserved to be the leader. He learned that lesson the hard way.

Years ago, when Reebok introduced the first aerobics shoe, people at Nike said, "That's bogus; we're not going to do that. It's not an athletic shoe." Three years later Nike was no longer the market leader. For a time in the late 1980s, Reebok was number one because Nike had said it didn't believe the aerobics shoe was ever going to catch on. There was no *competitive response*; there was just the decision that that wasn't Nike's business.

I think Phil Knight assimilated that lesson. You may not have to chase the business, but you need to do something. Even if you choose to ignore it, that's a decision you have to make, and that decision is something you are responsible for. There are plenty of things competitors did that we chose to ignore because we didn't think they were significant, but we always had to be aware of them and at least have the discussion about whether or not they were something that warranted our attention. So what your competitor does is never completely outside your boat.

"When a market condition changes or a competitive environment changes, those things are outside your control. But what you must control is your attention to them."

—LIZ DOLAN

"In business, your job is to control as many of the variables as you possibly can. You spend a lot of time trying to anticipate everything that could possibly happen. However, the economic situation can change, and that's outside your boat; the market condition can change, and that's outside your boat.

You can't really control what your competitors do, but it's your job to try to figure out what's about to happen and to react to it as quickly as you can. In business, nobody ever wants to admit that anything is outside their boat, because in an ideal business world you would control every variable. That's what you should try to do."

—LIZ DOLAN

4

Foster Creativity

LIZ DOLAN

President, Dolan St. Clair Sports Marketing
Consultants; creator and host of the *Satellite
Sisters* radio program on National Public Radio

IN BUSINESS YOU'RE REALLY TRAINED TO LISTEN to market conditions and to listen to what consumers want. That is definitely inside your boat. But in a creative process, it's actually very different. You try to keep market conditions outside your boat, because then the ultimate creative product is going to be more of what you want. If you integrate too much of the market thinking into your creative process, you just come up with something that sounds like everything else. I find it totally liberating to have huge categories of things that used to be in my boat totally outside my boat now. I love that.

IF YOU DON'T ROCK THE BOAT, YOU'LL BE DEAD IN THE WATER.

5

Unforeseen Waves May Carry You to Success

DAVID WOLPER
Award-winning movie and television producer

WHEN I PRODUCED *ROOTS*, I had no control over its programming. That was outside my boat. I got a call from Freddy Silverman at ABC, who said they were going to put *Roots* on every night in one week because they were afraid it might fail. In other words, if they got rid of it in one week and it failed, they'd lose only a week. They were telling me; they weren't asking me. That was something I had no control over.

I was stunned and said, "Are you sure you want to do it all in one week? Are people going to watch every night?" They didn't know the answer. They made their decision for the wrong reason. They figured that if it bombed they wouldn't screw up a time period for eight weeks.

It turned out the decision was perfect. It was ideal. People watched *Roots* night after night after night. The audience got bigger and bigger and bigger. The funny part is, it played the week before the ratings sweeps, so when it was all over, the affiliate stations went out of their minds. They wanted to know why the network hadn't started it the next week. It ran the last week in January, and it's still the highest-rated miniseries of all time.

As it turned out, the one thing I had no control over helped make *Roots* a big hit. It was huge, it was gigantic, it was one of the biggest hits in the history of television because it was on every night. Yet we all thought the network decision was crazy. That just proves that sometimes success is waiting for you outside your boat.

"I feel much more comfortable when I'm handling my own sword. There are a lot of independent businesspeople who are that way. They want to be in control. It's tough to surrender control. But sometimes you've got to do it and pass it on."

—JERRY SHAPIRO
Businessman, entrepreneur

6

Go with the Flow

JOHN DEBELLO
Movie producer, director, and writer

WE WERE SHOOTING our fourth cult film, *Killer Tomatoes Eat France*, with an all-French crew in Paris. The work ethic of the French crew and how they go about things is a lot different from an American crew's. For about a week I was trying to roll the rock uphill and enforce the same kind of speed and discipline and structure we have in the United States. But after about five days, I found myself falling further and further behind.

Finally we caught up and got a little ahead of schedule while filming at Notre Dame Cathedral. The crew went to eat lunch at a little café nearby. I said to the assistant director, who was an American, "You know what? Don't call them back after an hour. I want one of them to ask me, 'When will lunch be over?' I want to see if someone thinks it's close to an hour and he's ready to go back to work."

17

So they sat down for lunch, and after two hours, not a single person had even so much as looked at his watch. I realized I could be sitting there until midnight and no one would have given a damn. At that point, I just said, "Okay, the point is made. Call them back. We'll go to work."

After that, I didn't sweat the difference in the way the crew worked. It was totally out of my control. Life got a lot easier for the rest of the shoot. However, it took four or five days for me to figure out that I was going against a millennium of culture and not just a bunch of people who wanted to do things their way. It really was outside my boat. I finally realized that it was totally impossible to change the working habits of the French.

"We think the whole world is in our control, and none of it really is."

—JIM BERGLUND
General partner, Enterprise Partners Venture Capital

7

Create Fantasy by Excluding Reality

ROBERT TOWNE

Movie director and Oscar-winning
screenwriter of *Chinatown*

Wʜᴀᴛ's ɢᴇʀᴍᴀɴᴇ to the kind of proactive fatalism of "that's outside my boat" is the process you have to undergo as a writer, which is not only to know what is outside your boat, but to actively exclude it. In order to create fantasy, no matter how realistic it's based, you have to exclude reality. You cannot let those incursions come in, or they become more important than the fantasy. So part of writing is the discipline of keeping those things outside your boat that threaten your ability to deal with what's in it.

You do that by concentrating on what's inside your boat, which is to concentrate on what you've got. If you can't concentrate on the fantasy, it will never come to life. If you say, "Oh, I've got to return so-and-so's phone call, I've got to do this, I've got to do that, I've got to pick up the kids from school," these intrude on your boat, and you can't work. It doesn't mean you can't pick up your kids from school, but what it does mean is that unless at a certain point you are willing to recognize what's outside your boat, you will never be able to deal with what's in it.

Your mission as a writer, should you choose to accept it, is to go crazy, which is to live inside a fantasy. That's basically what the job is. It's to make the fantasy more real than the outside world or it'll never have any reality. If you can imagine this, everything outside your boat is reality and everything inside your boat is insanity. It takes a great deal of concentration to make the fantasy more vivid than the reality. You must do that or it will never come to life.

To be able to leave the boat is really a matter of imagining the boat to a point where you can afford to leave it and come back and it will be there. But you must get to the point of imagining the boat, of specifying it and all of its thwarts and gunnels and everything that you need. Once you can get to that point of imagining it, which means you have gone through a period of really excluding things, then you can traffic back and forth between what's outside it and what's inside it. It's risky, but it's quite doable. But until you get to that point you can't, because until then there is no boat.

**A SMOOTH SEA
NEVER PRODUCED
A SKILLFUL SAILOR.**

Celebrate What Is
Inside Your Boat

TOM SULLIVAN

Actor, athlete, singer, and motivational speaker
who has been blind since birth

B LINDNESS IS OUTSIDE MY BOAT, but what I have learned
is that the levels of available compensation far out-
strip the question of loss.

I'll take you on a quick journey. This morning, the
first thing that happened was that my guide dog,
Partner, licked my face and woke me up. That was my
first sensory experience of the day. Then there was a
bird, a robin in a tree outside the window, and I heard
that morning sound. I was still in bed. My wife, Patty,
was breathing quietly next to me, and I could absorb
every part of the fact that she was there—her smell, the
texture of her skin, everything. It's a place of love, and I
was there.

Then, outside the window, I smelled the fact that it was going to be a Santa Ana day because the wind was starting to blow in from the high desert. I smelled the ocean air and a patchy fog bank. I went downstairs and hit the button to make the coffee. It perked, and the sound of the perk meant morning was officially here. And the smell and taste of the coffee said, "Wake up."

Partner next guided me through the neighborhood, and I had a sense of oneness with the animal. We arrived where we run, along the strand at the beach. You can hear fifteen kinds of waves there, fifteen different ones, from the ones at high tide that come together with a dull thud to the ones at low tide that just ebb over the sandbar. That one has a long arc of sound.

As we ran, I smelled kelp, ocean air, and lilac. There's a restaurant that cooks breakfast nearby, and the smell of eggs and bacon came down and blended in. I heard from a distance the school bells, which I love. They say, "New day, children going to school." And at this time of year, the sea lions are in. As I ran harder, the sea lions became my crowd, and they lifted my level. I made believe they were in the stands applauding as I was running in the stadium with Partner.

All of that is to say, just in that microcosm, I can't change the stuff outside my boat, but I can relish and celebrate what's inside my boat. And that goes hand in hand with other things. I've never met an ugly person, because I can't see them. So ugliness for me is internal.

In terms of the system of labels, I've never carried levels of prejudice. I don't have racial questions ever; they've never been part of my life.

In terms of my sense of instinct, I use it to really hear what people are saying, rather than look past them. I'm of the conversation. When you and I are talking, as far as I'm concerned there is nothing else going on. When I look at all this in terms of my boat, I'm an able-bodied sailor inside my boat, and I love it.

I'm confirming that within the context of my life issue, my principal life issue, I'm very happy in my boat. Not just because I've accepted it—and this is the difference—not because I've accepted it but because I've celebrated it. There's a big difference between acceptance and celebration.

"You can talk to anybody who is truly well adjusted, and they like their boat."

—TOM SULLIVAN

"We have lost the perspective of being an American. We have become a selfish rather than a selfless society because people are saying, 'We'll take from the system rather than live inside our boat and be proud of what we are.'"

—TOM SULLIVAN

"I once went on a television casting call for Aaron Spelling, to appear on *Dynasty*. I was auditioning to play Linda Evans's love interest. The role was a blind country singer. Well, I'm not a country singer, but I went out and bought the boots and the jeans and the shirt, and I wrote a country song. I was totally prepared. I went in, and my performance absolutely killed them. I was tremendous.

"At the end of the audition, Mr. Spelling was sitting across the room and he said to his assistant, 'Oh, there's no way we can hire him. He's too good at being blind.' That was his line! Then he added, 'We need a sighted guy to fake it.' Now, that was really outside my boat."

—TOM SULLIVAN

9

Never Lose Sight of Where You Want to Land

CANDY LEE

President and CEO, Troll Communications

I<small>T'S EASIER FOR PEOPLE TO PINPOINT THE ERROR</small> of small things, so that even though we believe in letting people make their own decisions, we tend to second-guess them in things that don't really matter. For example, we can fixate on a minor issue, such as a color change, instead of asking if this change affects the bottom line. One thing that's outside my boat is the minor details that don't make enough difference to a customer. There is no need for me to micromanage.

For almost all managers it's easier to focus on the small details than it is to manage the bigger picture. Many managers get sidetracked into small things because they're finite, they're specific, such changes are easy to suggest and they make a difference when you do them.

However, these things may not be worth enough for the amount of effort involved to do them. These small things should be outside the manager's boat.

Nonetheless, it's hard to leave small things outside your boat because they're so easy to pick up. The smaller something is, the more likely you are to say that that change can be done. Because it's easy you tend to want to do it, but you must leave it and concentrate on the more difficult things that are harder to see. You need to focus on the bigger picture.

I actually think that when you're running a company most things are in your boat, and if you don't manage the growth of the company so it can reach its goals, then you're not doing your job. I believe that making sure the boat is pointed in the right direction to reach its destination in the most efficient way and to deliver the best bottom line is what being in the boat is all about.

You may not understand how to get the fuel into the tanks or how to hoist the sails, but making sure that the boat is going to reach the harbor at a price that delivers money to the bottom line is the captain's job.

"Everything that creates customer satisfaction is
within all of our boats. If we only take our job
detail to the boundary of our department and we
don't ensure that the ultimate customer has an
experience that is beneficial, then we haven't
advanced the cause."

—CANDY LEE

"People in business spend a lot of time trying
to fix things instead of just moving on. You have
to be quick to admit that the conditions have
changed, but oftentimes you get so emotionally
attached to a decision you made a year ago under
different conditions that you can't move on."

—DONNA DUBINSKY
Cofounder and CEO, Handspring

**FOLLOW YOUR
INNER COMPASS.**

10

Focus On Your Boat

MARK CUBAN
Internet billionaire and
owner of the NBA Dallas Mavericks

WHAT YOU CALL "OUTSIDE MY BOAT" is what we in the Internet world call "drowning in opportunity." At Broadcast.com, Todd Wagner, my cofounder, and I were constantly deluged by ideas. In an industry where every idea seemed to be earmarked for billions of dollars, everyone had plenty of ideas to go around.

Broadcast.com had more than a hundred salespeople, and it seemed as if not a day went by that our salespeople wouldn't bring back a "great idea" from someone they were trying to do business with. It got to the point where we would have to hold meetings to remind our salespeople of some very important qualifications and criteria to apply when dealing with prospects. They were: (1) Were they going to pay cash? (2) How soon would they pay? If the answers weren't "yes" and "within ninety days," then we made it clear that the salesperson was wasting his or her time.

We were already working on developing Broadcast.com into *the* broadcast network on the Internet, and that "everything else" could have led to our drowning. Focus was the key to our success.

"What's outside your boat is when you're humming along with your technology, thinking you're doing great with the intellectual property you're developing, and you find out that there's some other guy in a garage someplace who's beat you to the punch. Suddenly they're in the market and you're not. That's outside your boat. You just can't know that. You try to know, but sometimes you can't."

—JIM BERGLUND
General partner, Enterprise Partners Venture Capital

11

Chart Your Own Course

COLLEEN MOOREHEAD
President, E*Trade Canada

O NE OF MY MENTORS, whom I met about fifteen years ago, told me that when somebody asks you how you are, say that you're great. The reason you do this is that by saying so, you can really make yourself feel great. And by focusing on the positives and the things you can control, your ability to be successful and achieve your goals is much more likely because you're starting with the right mental set.

I had the opportunity to launch E*Trade, an on-line financial service, in Canada. It's a very strong brand in the U.S. market, but in Canada it had many of the characteristics of a start-up organization, where people were rewarded for taking risks and building. I left a very comfortable, traditional organization for this start-up opportunity.

We started doing business in a market where our competitors were large Canadian banks that had been formed through an act of Parliament 135 years ago. We had to make sure we focused on the things that were inside our boat. In the early days we were resource constrained. We had to build a brand in Canada, and that was tough work. We had to be creative. We had to have breakthrough marketing messages. We were rebels.

We like to think we've learned as much through the things we've done wrong as the things we've done right. When you're a new organization you make mistakes. You have to. If you ever create a culture where you stop making mistakes, then you become the bad guys. You're not letting people take risks, and you're not going to experience those breakthroughs.

The environment was what the environment was; it was outside our boat, but we had to deal with it. We responded to it. We couldn't change the market conditions; the market conditions were what they were. We had to work as a team. When we had a problem, we'd "swarm it." We'd get a group of people together, and everyone could bring a suggestion to solve the problem. This isn't hierarchical; it's interdisciplinarian. One of us would say, "This is a big problem we have to solve." What results is different thinking, which creates a breakthrough. And that breakthrough is what enables us to deal with the environment, because we collectively have to solve it.

We also tried to keep our competitors outside our boat. We needed to have knowledge of them; I certainly wouldn't want to drive a car with my hands over my eyes. But if we did what our competitors did or responded as our competitors did, we gained no competitive advantage. Our opportunity came from understanding what our strengths were and from using those strengths in the competitive environment.

Our focus was to do things electronically, to do them first, and to do so positioned as a customer advocate, which meant that customers should be able to do everything themselves. So, for instance, if I hadn't kept my traditional Canadian competitors outside my boat, I would have built branches, because all the banks had branches. But that wouldn't be E*Trade. We were developing a different way to have a bricks-and-mortar relationship, one that could occur through a strategic alliance.

I didn't think business could be this enjoyable. I work with people who have fun, we have a culture that we nurture and hold on to, and we all protect it. We're very proud of our rebellious streak.

"If you let any day go by that you don't try to affect your success, you've missed a day. You can never get it back."

—COLLEEN MOOREHEAD

"You can't control how your competitors compete. You can have strategies against your competitors, but you can't make their decisions for them. You have to go in assuming that they're great competitors, because if you don't, you can't win."

—COLLEEN MOOREHEAD

WINNING IS OUTSIDE YOUR BOAT; PREPARING TO WIN IS INSIDE YOUR BOAT.

You Can Sail Against Economic Winds

JIM BURDICK
President and CEO, Unique Technologies

FOUNDING A START-UP COMPANY in the worst downturn in the history of the business might not be the smartest thing to do. But that's what we did. In 1997, we started Unique Technologies, a hired-gun sales and marketing force for emerging semiconductor companies that don't have their own sales forces. We're electrical engineers who sell semiconductor products to companies such as Cisco, Lucent, Nortel, and QUALCOMM. We also have a distribution operation that houses the semiconductor chips we sell.

We formed the company in a very severe downturn in the industry when things were really not very good. But I think when you're starting a company in that environment you learn to operate with a very lean management structure. Company culture is extremely important, as is disseminating that culture to the people who work for you. You build the company person by person, and if you hire a good one, that good one will find another good one. We built it deliberately, person by person, and operated in that mode for the first three years. When the industry took off in the year 2000, our sales went through the roof.

The downturn in the economy was outside our boat, so we just tried to control what was inside our boat. The first year we recorded $45 million in sales, the next year $102 million, then $236 million, then $460 million. We grew 100 percent per year for four years. This year, our fifth, we'll do a billion dollars.

We have stayed tightly focused. While our competitors carry two hundred lines, we carry twelve. Because of this approach, we have no ambiguity about where we're going, what we're doing, and what products we sell. We're not just floating around waiting for things to happen. Although our employee count has grown from 50 to 210, it hasn't increased as much as we originally thought it would because we are very focused on the types of customers we call on.

Another thing we do is to pay more than a fair wage. We're willing to pay more for experience and for the people who make up the team. Their value is just huge. One person will do the job of three when the strategy is set right. We also put a tremendous amount of emphasis on the engineers and engineering sales technical people, as opposed to our competitors, who think of the engineers as merely the cost of doing business. We look at it as an investment in the business that absolutely pays off.

Starting a business during the worst economic downturn in history can be the death knoll for many investors. But if you understand what is completely outside your control and choose to spend your time, energy, and creativity on what you can control—what's inside your boat—economic success will follow.

"There is business out there, there is demand for the products out there. The economy will surge, and it will advance and it will fall back. Once you've established your game plan, make sure all your players know exactly what to do. Keep your cost structure set up so you can take the downturns. When the upturns happen, the profit is just huge. But you've got to be able to operate when the economy slows down."

—JIM BURDICK

"Our best new hires have been men who commanded nuclear submarines. They are intelligent and good at multitasking, and they really love the team environment. In addition, we can give them very small offices without windows."

—JIM BURDICK

13

Sometimes It Pays to Toss Things Overboard

RON GIDWITZ
Former CEO, Helene Curtis

WHEN I TOOK OVER AT HELENE CURTIS, the company had not been doing particularly well. We had been engaged in a lot of short-term planning. We'd come out with one mediocre product after another. Each would be in the market for a while, and then it would disappear. Our businesses were extremely diverse. We were in the plastics business. We were in the adhesives business. We were in the door-to-door cosmetics business. We were in the fragrance business. Finally we realized this didn't make any sense at all. We had to live our business life a different way.

So we sat down and did a thorough assessment of our strengths and our weaknesses. We determined that what we did know how to do well was develop hair care products; we really didn't know how to do all that other stuff.

We decided to put all our resources into what we were really good at and get out of all the businesses that didn't make any sense. We put together a strategic plan that essentially said we would build our hair care business one step at a time.

First we focused on Suave. It was a great success. Then we spent a bunch of time and money in our R-and-D labs. We created Finesse Conditioner, which was a fabulous product. We basically bet the company on developing hair care product brands. We spent a fortune on advertising. What we really did was focus our assets on what we knew, and we rid ourselves of all the extraneous businesses, that were really outside our boat.

The strength inside our boat was hair care products, so that's where we focused our resources and energy. In all candor, we started to concentrate on this business only in the late 1980s, and Helene Curtis brands will soon have the second largest market share in the country after Procter & Gamble.

"Never mistake activity for achievement."

—BILL WALTON
Hall of Fame basketball player

14

Secure All Hatches

RON GIDWITZ
Former CEO, Helene Curtis

I CAN REMEMBER HAVING DINNER with Sam Walton of Wal-Mart years ago. He drove up in his red pick-up truck, the proverbial red pick-up truck. His strategy and our Suave strategy were identical—high-quality products at low prices—so we really had a leg up with Wal-Mart. We absolutely took advantage of that. We built our Suave business on it, using Wal-Mart as our major partner.

As Wal-Mart grew, the people there became very focused on how they could continue to drive the cost of products down, not just by buying at a good price, but also by perfecting the logistics. They became very smart buyers, and they became very demanding on their suppliers to deliver 100 percent of what they wanted on time. On time meant to the hour, delivered to whichever warehouse they wanted it, complete. No back orders, no mistakes. They wanted the trucks to roll up at the appointed hour with all the merchandise.

We found we weren't good enough. We couldn't perform at that level. Keep in mind that Wal-Mart represents about 25 percent of the business of most consumer-oriented companies. It's really important. We were in danger of losing its business because we couldn't service it within the parameters they insisted upon.

What we needed to do was be creative. We formed a special group for Wal-Mart with a separate warehouse and a separate distribution and logistics organization. All this special group did was take care of Wal-Mart. We ran it for a little over a year, and we learned to service Wal-Mart perfectly.

Next we took all the lessons we learned from our Wal-Mart experience and applied them to the rest of our organization. As a result we became one of the best service providers in the consumer business. It all started because we moved Wal-Mart's performance criteria from outside our boat to inside our boat.

"Business problems are like being thrown into the sea and realizing you can either tread water to stay afloat or focus all your energy on swimming to shore."

—ANOUSHEH ANSARI
Cofounder, Telecom Technologies

**ALWAYS BE ON
THE LOOKOUT FOR A
LIGHTHOUSE AND
A SAFE HARBOR.**

15

Don't Give Up the Ship

BUD GRAVETTE

Former chairman and CEO, the Bowery Savings Bank

T HERE WERE MANY TIMES in my business career when it
would have been easier to walk away from a tough
situation and not look into every possible venue for a
solution. Whenever I was given the response "We can't
do that!" my first reaction was to immediately find out
why we couldn't do whatever it was we were attempting
to accomplish.

A situation developed while I was in New York City
at the time of the thrift industry problems. It was during
my tenure as the chairman and CEO of the Bowery
Savings Bank, a venerable thrift institution almost 150
years old. We were given one of those intolerable
answers to something we were trying to do: "It's against
the law. You can't do that!" Instead of walking away
from a prospective resolution because the law wouldn't
allow it, we presented our position to Mickey Siebert,
the superintendent of banks for the State of New York.

Following a review of the opportunity, her response was what might have been expected from this experienced and astute businessperson. Ms. Siebert agreed that something should be done, and she said, "Let's go to the legislature and change the law!" Together we did just that, and the law was changed.

The alternative is not to bail out because of a negative response to a problem, but instead to find a positive way to resolve the issue. If the law has to be changed, then change it. I'm a great believer that if you got into the boat in the first place, the last place you want to be is in the water!

"The only philosophy of life that is compatible with sanity is optimism. You can't really succeed unless you are optimistic and have self-confidence. If you lose confidence in yourself, you're done."

—SUMNER REDSTONE
CEO, Viacom

16

Believe In Your Boat

DR. IRWIN JACOBS
CEO and chairman of the board, QUALCOMM

WE BEGAN TO PAY ATTENTION to code division technology in the fall of 1988. We originally looked at it for satellite application, but we later wondered if we could use it for cellular. Then, in January 1989, the whole industry voted on a selection of technology for moving to digital cellular from what had been analog cellular. There were two choices, FDMA and TDMA, neither of which was our technology. Ours was called CDMA.

The decision was hard-fought and controversial, but finally it was made. Just as the industry was settling down to work on the chosen technology, TDMA, we felt confident enough to approach the industry and say, "Hey, there is another way to do this: CDMA." Of course, that was not well received by many because of the long fight that had just taken place.

We made a presentation in June 1989. Nobody found any holes in what we were saying, so we went ahead with our plan to make a major demonstration in November. Others had looked at various approaches to this type of technology, but they had never been able to make it work properly. This technology was outside their boat, but it was entirely inside our boat.

We decided that the only way to convince others that CDMA would work, since many had tried unsuccessfully, was to invite a large group to come to our San Diego headquarters and kick the tires, give it a try.

We worked very hard for several months to develop a demonstration of the technology. We weren't quite ready, but we decided to go ahead anyway and invite people to visit, since we had to give them about a six-week lead time. All this was done in twelve months from initial concept to demonstration. We basically had things ready to go when everybody showed up. We began our presentation with a few speakers, and then I came on to describe what was going to happen, what they would see, what they could try.

The intent was to break up the group; some would remain in the building, talking over a mobile telephone through CDMA technology, and others would go in a van and be able to drive around, also talking over this new system. But I began to get signals from the back of the room that the system wasn't working and I'd better stall. So I kept talking. Luckily I'd been a university professor, so finding ways to fill time was within my boat.

About forty-five minutes later I finally got a signal that it was okay to send groups out. Sure enough, everything went ahead successfully. But that was one of those times where just a few minutes either way could have made a major difference.

For the most part, that was the beginning of the acceptance of the technology. However, even after it was in operation, people were still saying that either it wouldn't work or it was going to have a problem for the next several years. But we held tight to our belief in the technology. We were confident of what was in our boat, and we weren't going to toss it overboard. Now, looking forward, just about everybody says that CDMA is the correct technology, and even if they haven't used it to date, they will be using it in their next generation products.

"Great leaders can create a vision and say, 'This is what's in our boat right now.' And people will jump inside and shout, 'Let's go, let's go!' They want to get in that boat."

—MICHAEL MCNEAL
Vice president of business development,
PureCarbon, Inc.

**FLOAT YOUR
OWN BOAT.**

Look Out for
Storm Warnings

GEORGE MONTGOMERY

Former president and CEO, TaylorMade Golf;
senior vice president of sales and marketing,
K2 Corporation

O NE OF THE THINGS I'VE OBSERVED working in the sports business is that all sports are cyclical. They grow and they retract, depending on environmental and economic conditions, and those conditions are completely out of the control of any executive within that particular sport. What you see is a rapid growth in participation and spending or a rapid decline in participation and spending.

For example, in the ski business in 1991, there was very little snow and then short-term interest rates skyrocketed. The next year very few people spent money on new ski equipment. There was about a 37 percent decline in the overall ski market. As one company within that market, there's very little you can do about it. You've just got to ride with the tide, and your boat is floating as the tide either comes in or goes out.

The first thing you have to do is accept the fact that you can't control the overall economic conditions and to some degree you can't control the overall market size. But you can control how you respond to them within the company. What you need to do is identify the early storm warning signals and pay close attention to them.

In both the ski business and the golf business, you could have a swing in the overall market of plus or minus 20 percent year to year, but you have to have your eyes open to anticipate it. You're in the best situation if you can see it coming before your competitors do. You can adjust your inventories, adjust your level of trade receivables risk, and plan your spending if you know what your market potential is going to be.

If the storm warning in the ski business is snowfall, in the golf business it is sell-through at retail. We would check to see how quickly our clubs were selling to consumers through the retail channel. As soon as that slowed down for two months in a row, our warning bells would go off and we would start adjusting our spending and adjusting our production levels.

In the golf business in 1998, the overall market dropped a little over 20 percent for clubs in one year, and that was after five years of double-digit growth. It just turned on its heels and retracted. Most of our competitors weren't ready for it. At TaylorMade we reacted early in the season and cut our production plans. We watched our inventory, and we watched the credit we gave out for trade receivables because we knew our retailers would have a hard time. As a result we ended up the year profitable while some of our major competitors lost more than $40 million. It's a matter of watching for the early storm warnings and then reacting very quickly.

The other take-away is that when you don't control the overall market, you have to swallow your pride. You can't take too much credit when the market's healthy and your company is growing, and you can't internalize too much blame when the market retracts. All you can do is control your business within the market.

Inside your boat you identify the early storm warnings and then identify the critical areas of inventory risk, receivables risk, and your spending. You can control all three of these. And the faster you respond to the storm warnings, the better off you are.

"Your business, the model and plan, changes almost quarterly—at times, daily. You've got to anticipate and adapt to every shift in the landscape."

—LAURA GROPPÉ
Chairman and CEO, Girl Games

18

Don't Be Afraid to Change Boats

CAMERON HALL

Former senior marketing manager, Coca-Cola and
Monsanto; now a management consultant

IN BUSINESS TODAY, you have a lot more options than you think you have. You're in your boat, but you can be in another boat in a second. When you go to work for a company these days, you sign a contract with yourself as opposed to signing a contract to work for a company. Therefore, if you feel trapped in your boat, you can leave that boat at any time, but be sure to take your toolbox of skills and knowledge with you.

Most people get into a job and they stay in that job way too long. They're unhappy. It affects their personal life, it affects their friends, it affects how they work. They start learning more and more about less and less, and they're really not adding value to the company anymore. They know it. They may not have been discovered yet, but they know that someday they're going to be discovered, and it gets to be a miserable existence. This is the time to fire yourself.

At Monsanto, I was the worldwide head of consumer products. I was a very good operator, and because I was a very good operator, they graduated me into a senior staff job. Although I was good at the staff job, I really didn't like it. It entailed resetting policy and implementing it with four hundred people who were working for me in eighty countries. I was the master of none, but I set policy. I made decisions on the direction of the company. But this was not what I wanted to do. I didn't perceive that I was adding a lot of value. It got to a point when we sold one of our companies that I had the opportunity to basically fire myself—ask for a package, ask to get out. So I did.

Leaving your boat like that can be scary, especially if it's the first time you've done it. You ask yourself, "Do I have the skills to add value in the next business I enter so that people will reward me, or is this going to be it?" I think most people who live in the corporate world carry a fear that when they leave their job, it's the end. They'll never be able to return to the position they had previously. They'll never be compensated at that same level.

After some retrospection, I found that when you fire yourself from a job, you go out with dignity; you go out with your personal esteem intact. You discover very rapidly that you will carry the skills and knowledge you have into your next job. Remember: leave the boat, but don't forget your toolbox.

For instance, I didn't actually realize how skilled a marketer I was until I left Monsanto. I spent about eight months getting my personal affairs in order, reconnecting with my family, and then I joined E*Trade Canada, where I believed I could add enormous value. I had a new confidence level that having done it once, I could do it again. I worked at E*Trade Canada for eighteen to twenty months, and when it was appropriate, I hired my successor and fired myself again. I'm much happier and I feel much more rewarded in a job when I know I'm adding a lot of value.

It takes a lot of guts to say, "You know what? I'm leaving the boat." But it's not the end of the world. Take your toolbox with you, and head off in a new direction. Even if it's not perfectly right, pick a direction and go, because there are hundreds of opportunities out there. Go where you can add value, and things will be fine. This is the way to enjoy life's journey.

"Don't wait for someone to discover you're not adding value; you know first. When you discover that about yourself, have the guts to stand up and say, 'You know what? I'm going to move on to something else.' Your confidence should come from the experiences you've built and from your toolbox."

—CAMERON HALL

**FIND A BOAT
THAT'S GOING IN
YOUR DIRECTION
AND JUMP ON
BOARD.**

19

Be Ready to Alter Your Course

ARTHUR BLANK

Cofounder, The Home Depot

Bernie Marcus and I were two highly successful Los Angeles businessmen. Under our management, The Handy Dan Home Improvement Centers—there were sixty-six of them grossing $155 million in sales—had become one of the nation's most respected and successful home improvement chains. Handy Dan was 81 percent owned by the Daylin Corporation and 19 percent owned by public stock.

Even with the success of the Handy Dan centers, the Daylin Corporation was struggling, so its CEO, "Sandy" Sigoloff, decided to buy back the public stock. This would give him complete control of all of Daylin Corporation's subsidiaries. In a battle of egos, not only did he do this, but he then immediately fired both Bernie Marcus and me. The filing of lawsuits on both sides immediately followed.

However, Bernie and I soon realized that the firing was truly something over which we had no control. So instead of wasting any more time with it, we decided to get on with our lives and try something totally new. We'd see where it would take us. Our friend Ken Langone, an investment banker, told us, "You've just been kicked in the ass with a golden horseshoe. This is the greatest opportunity because now you can open the business you have always dreamed of."

Our vision was an immense warehouse store, up to 75,000 square feet with very high ceilings. We would buy direct from the manufacturers and pass on the savings to our customers. There would be a tremendous amount of merchandise with a great assortment stacked from floor to ceiling, offering bargains for all.

For starters, we approached Ross Perot for a $2 million investment in return for 70 percent of our new company. There was interest on both sides, but we weren't a compatible group and thus we were unable to work anything out. Instead, our investment banker was able to raise the $2 million through several investors, and we had to give up only 50 percent of the company. We were now ready to get under way.

We named our new company the Home Depot. Just how successful have we been by putting our firing from Handy Dan outside our boat and concentrating on what we could control? Well, let's put it this way: the $2 million that Ross Perot did not invest in the original 70 pecent share of Home Depot stock would be worth about $58 billion today. That's right, $58 billion.

"Most people think companies are successful; but there are no successful companies in America. Only people can be successful."

—TED OWEN
President and publisher, the *San Diego Business Journal*

"Being laid off is a little bit like getting thrown out of a boat. You know you can swim, but you don't know exactly how far the shore is."

—MIKE O'CONNOR
Former vice president of operations for a retail chain

20

Set Sail

DION JULIAN LATTIMORE
CFO and president, Dion Scott,
Custom Wardrobe Designers

O PENING OUR OWN BUSINESS required a total leap of
faith. My partner, Scott Torrellas, and I had just
been fired from our previous job at a men's clothing
store. We had no control over that even though we had
been their leading salesmen. We didn't have any money,
and we didn't have any tailors to make any clothes.
Nonetheless, we couldn't worry about that because there
was rent to pay and a car note that was due. We just had
to create some way of opening our own business.

We could be concerned only with what we could
control, what was inside our boat, and that was just to
get started. We went to a local fabric store in downtown
Los Angeles and cut swatches from fifty different bolts
of fabric and put together our own swatch book. Then

we went to the hotel where the Houston Rockets were staying, and we ended up selling $50,000 in clothes to NBA players that day. That's how we began.

The first player I sold a suit to was Kenny Smith. I said, "Look, Kenny, we don't have any tailors to make this and we can't even tell you when you might get them back, but if you just trust us, in six weeks we're going to have some nice clothes for you." He said, "If you can make me clothes like you have in the past, I'll stay with you." He did, and he referred us to Hakeem Olajuwon and a few others, and that's what launched Dion Scott.

We started working out of my apartment, and when we finally got our store on Robertson it stayed vacant for almost four months. We were working on cardboard boxes and a phone from my house, and UPS wouldn't even come to the office, because they didn't think our business was open. Half the time we had to run down the street to catch the driver to get our shipments.

In our first year we did $1 million in sales, and we doubled that number the second year. We've been in business six years, and we have well over two thousand clients in forty-eight states. We're opening a store in New York City, and we're launching our ready-to-wear line. The company is growing and we're operating in the black because we take care of what is inside our boat.

"Probably some of the best folks I ever worked with were people who had learned a lot from their mistakes. It is the people who don't learn who scare me. I'd love to know that you got fired and what you learned from that because you could be very valuable to saving my company from making those same mistakes."

—MICHAEL MCNEAL
Vice president of business development,
PureCarbon, Inc.

"We don't have control over how an organization handles a layoff, but we do have control over how we choose as individuals to respond to it."

—MICHELLE L. REINA
Coauthor of *Trust and Betrayal in the Workplace*

21

Focus on Performance, Not Outcome

JOHN GULICK

Director of communications, Computer Sciences
Corporation; author of *Media Isn't a Four Letter Word*

I DID A TWENTY-YEAR TOUR in the Air Force, and it was my experience that people who were successful didn't worry about making sure they attended all the right schools or had all the right jobs. Because when they concentrated on just that, they found out they were disappointed more often than not. But when people said, "Ah, the hell with it. I'm just going to do what I do best," they were very successful. They got promoted.

People who concentrated so much on doing what the system dictated penalized themselves in the long run. Disappointed, they would finally say, "Ah, that's outside my boat. I'm not going to get promoted anyway, so I'll just do what I want to do." Ironically, as soon as they did that, they got promoted.

For example, there were a lot of people who said, "I want to be a United States Air Force Thunderbird pilot." They dedicated their lives to it. For the most part, the ones who did that didn't make it. But the pilot who went out and did the best possible job he could at flying and at being a good officer and a good citizen made it. It wasn't an obsession with him. He just lived his life to the best of his abilities, and success came his way.

"If you don't give up, if you keep on trying, if you keep being positive, if you keep moving forward, good things will happen."

—DAVID HAKOLA
Sales associate, Brothers International Desserts

"Life is like a ten-speed bike. Most of us have gears we never use."

—CHARLES SCHULZ
Creator of *Peanuts*

Overcome and Adapt

TED OWEN

President and publisher of the *San Diego Business Journal*; former Marine captain, retired (Mustang)

T HE MARINE CORPS TEACHES LEADERSHIP at every level in the military, and one of the Marine Corps' favorite sayings is "Overcome and Adapt." If you're given a challenge or the responsibility to do something and it's not in your purview, you either have to overcome that or you adapt by finding some other way to do it.

A young lieutenant, on temporary duty from the Marine Barracks in Pearl Harbor, is a perfect example of that saying. He had been in Vietnam for just two weeks as an artillery forward observer. His job was to locate targets and call for and adjust artillery fire.

His company was on patrol on the Anderson Trail, south of Da Nang, when it got hit. Enemy soldiers were popping up out of spider holes in the ground and seemed to be everywhere. The Marines were pinned down by extremely accurate enemy fire. Their company commander was mortally wounded and the radio operator was dead. The lieutenant then realized he was the ranking officer.

He immediately assumed command of the rifle company and moved at once into the midst of the heavy fire. He led their attack on enemy positions from which deadly fire continued to come. His sound and swift decisions served to stabilize his units.

He moved through enemy fire using two armed helicopters to control an air attack, while at the same time directing one platoon in a successful counterattack to a key enemy position. He also directed helicopters for the evacuation of the dead and wounded.

This young lieutenant had been placed in a position of extreme stress. He was completely outside his boat. He had not been trained as an infantry officer. This was his first time in Vietnam. He was there on temporary duty, yet he was able to "overcome and adapt." For his heroic actions on that day, Lt. Harvey C. Barnum Jr., an artillery forward observer, was awarded the Medal of Honor, our nation's highest award for heroism, by the president of the United States.

"It turns out there are some pretty remarkable physical and mental feats humans can do when they decide to try. We don't know what the limits are. What we know is the limits haven't been touched yet."

—ED HUBBARD
USAF colonel, retired

"Man doesn't know what he is capable of until he is asked."

—KOFI ANNAN
United Nations Secretary-General

**ROW THE BOAT
YOU'RE GIVEN.**

23

Discover What Is Important

ED MECHENBIER

Major General U.S. Air Force Reserve; Vietnam
prisoner of war for six years; corporate vice president,
Science Applications International Corporation

I WAS ON A BOMBING MISSION in an F-4 about thirty miles northeast of Hanoi when I managed to run my airplane into a barrage of flak. It caught fire and wasn't flying anymore, so I jumped out on Flag Day 1967 and spent the next 2,100 days in North Vietnam.

You're trained, as a military aviator, for survival situations, but when you're actually put into one for real, all of your training goes out the window. There's no preparation for the reality of being surrounded by fire in an airplane that is no longer flying. You're normally taught to take off, land, and do things inside an airplane. You're not taught to operate in an environment where there is no flying left, you're just tumbling through the sky and

70

the most prominent scene on the horizon for everybody to see is a fireball. All of a sudden the ejection seat comes out of that fireball.

I was no longer a pilot. I'd been through survival training, and I'd been through jungle survival and water survival, but when I actually landed and there were people there with a lot more guns than I'd ever seen in one place at one time and they were all pointing at me, well, that was outside my boat. I hadn't been there before. So you just go along and you adapt, and that's what matters.

You discover the resilience of the human body and of the human spirit. Here I am all of a sudden, I'm scared to death. Five minutes ago I was a knight in shining armor charging windmills and knocking them all down. Now I've got a bunch of people who are at least a whole foot shorter than I am, but they've got the guns and I'm going where they tell me to go.

You don't have a choice. You don't get to raise your hand and say, "King's X." You just have to absorb what they give you. If somebody were to tell you, "I'm going to take you out and I'm going to hit you fifty, sixty, seventy times with a fan belt," you'd say, "What? No, I can't handle that. Something bad will happen." But after sixty, seventy, or one hundred whacks, you're still there. You say, "Yes, I can do this." They take your hands and manacle them behind your back. You know the drill. They're going to rotate your hands up over your shoulders and dislocate both your shoulders, and the next thing you know you're going to see your hands back to back in front of your face, having rotated over. It's a hard thing to imagine. But at the moment you're going through it, you just adapt to it. It hurts, but that's outside your boat. You can't control it. You can't say, "Oh, that's far enough. Stop now, please." That's not an option.

The only way you could personalize it would be to get mad at the people who are doing it to you. That's the only outlet you have. But they're just doing their job. The war for me was not a personal thing against them individually. They were doing what somebody told them to do. You're still in combat. He's still your enemy; you're still his enemy; and you're both trying to do a job. He just has you outnumbered, that's all. If you ever let it get to you in that sense, you'll just cave and do anything they want you to do.

You always understand that no matter how uncomfortable your personal situation is, you're never alone. You've got a bunch of other guys in there who are counting on you to do the best you can, and they're expecting you to do the best you can. That's a pretty powerful thing. It's the same thing in football. If ten guys do their job and one doesn't, the play's a bust, no matter how beautifully those other ten do their job. It sounds a little hokey, but I really think that's the attitude we had: I may be the only POW in this cell block right now, I may be the only guy the Vietnamese are beating on right now, but what I do sets a tone. I don't give them the information they may use on somebody else. We never lost sight of the fact that we were part of a team.

I spoke to a cancer group the other night, people with brain tumors, and they were all dwelling on the torture part of being a POW. I said, "Time out. The torture, like your sickness, is a very small percent of the day-to-day problems. Your life goes on, our life went on. If torture was two percent, five percent or ten percent of the time we were there, then that's the part people hear about. It's all the other things that happen—the funny things, the personal things, the interaction you have with the people you live with inside the cell, how well you get to know yourself inside the cell. The rest of the time is where the real learning or the real strength comes from. It's like a long religious retreat. You get to know yourself and the people around you, and you get to find out what it's like to do something above and beyond your individual talents."

What we went through helps you identify the things that are important in your life. It helps you put things into perspective and to figure out what's in your boat and what's not in your boat. Then you tend to spend your time on the important things, not ignoring the unimportant things but recognizing them for what they are.

I told the people in the cancer group, "When you compare what you're going through to what I went through, although the physical environment may be different and the consequences may be different, mentally it's all the same. You're struggling to do something that's important."

———

"When I ejected out of that fireball I was almost out of time. It's one and three quarters seconds from the time you pull the ejection handle until you have a parachute—a full parachute. Before my parachute opened my airplane hit the ground. So, I wake up every morning and I say, 'Thank you, God.' I'm literally one of those guys who came within two seconds of not being here."

—ED MECHENBIER

"Since I returned from Vietnam, I've had bad minutes, but never a bad day."

—ED MECHENBIER

See the Silver Lining

ED HUBBARD

Colonel, U.S. Air Force, retired;
Vietnam prisoner of war for
six years, seven months, twelve days

I WAS VERY FORTUNATE. As a POW, I lived with a man in prison who gave me a great piece of advice several years before I was released. I sat down and thought about it, and I adopted his philosophy. He said that what we were receiving was the most expensive education we would ever get, and we'd already paid the price, so now we must reap the rewards. He added that the day you leave prison you must put all the horrors behind you, all of the things over which you have no control, and you must take back nothing but the good things you learned here. Go home and use those to improve the rest of your life. He said that to me approximately three years before I was released, so I had a long time to mentally prepare myself to do just that.

It sounds relatively simple until you try it. When I came home, the very first day I was back in the United States, I met my wife, who was twenty-three years old when I was shot down and thirty when I returned. She had become a world-class alcoholic. I stood there that first day and I saw this wonderful person whom I had left, who had destroyed her life because she hated and she couldn't put the horrors behind her. I lived with her for six and a half years after I came home, and I watched her walk down that road—the other option. She couldn't let it go. She died when she was thirty-nine years old. She literally drank herself to death. So not only did I have outstanding advice before I came home, I had a great reminder every day of my life after I came home that this was not the direction to go.

I got into public speaking quite by accident, but I believe it's probably the single greatest therapy on earth. Shrinks will tell you, if you've got a problem, talk about it. I have the privilege of talking about it every day and I get paid to do it, which is rather remarkable when you think about it. Instead of me paying some shrink a lot of money so I can talk to him, somebody else pays me to talk. The benefit, besides what I personally receive, is that I get a thousand letters and e-mails a year from people who are in the audience, who swear I have completely changed their life. People who are struggling and trying to deal with horrors in their lives. I gave them a concept they've applied that's worked. I get letters from people I spoke to ten years ago who say they've never had a bad day since. The rewards are immense on a daily basis.

I never had to go through that difficult decision tree: Am I going to deal with this as a positive or a negative? But I can tell you, there are some people I was with in prison who haven't accepted it quite that well. About three years ago, I was up in Duluth, Minnesota, to speak, and without my knowledge they had slipped another former POW into the audience. I didn't know he was there. I finished my speech, and he came walking up out of the crowd. I immediately knew him; I had lived with him in the same cell. I said, "Hi, Dave, how are you doing?" He replied, "I have a question. Are you sure you and I were in the same prison together? I didn't learn any of those things."

I went to dinner with him and his wife that night, and the next day they took me to the airport. He dropped us off at check-in, and while he was parking the car his wife gave me a big hug. She said, "You will never, ever know how important it was for you to come to town and tell that story, because Dave has been fighting and struggling with a lot of bitterness ever since he came home. And after you left last night, we sat down and had a four-hour discussion about how fortunate we were. We had been looking at the world through the wrong set of eyes."

To be able to take a guy who was there, who could understand all this but hadn't quite figured it out, and set his life back on track was really a very great opportunity. That's what I do for a living, and I tell you what, it doesn't get any better than this.

"There's something that Americans desperately need to know—we have within us a tremendous amount of opportunity, physically and mentally, to change and improve the world."

—ED HUBBARD

"I've been called by more than one person an arrogant bastard, but I say, 'No, I'm not arrogant. I just know I can do things you can't do. And the only reason I can do them and you can't is because I believe I can do them and you don't believe you can.'"

—ED HUBBARD

CAN YOU IMAGINE
WHAT WOULD HAPPEN
IF EVERYONE WOULD
ROW IN THE SAME
DIRECTION FOR
ONE DAY?

25

Control What You Can Control

WILLIE DAVIS

NFL Hall of Fame, Green Bay Packers;
president and CEO, All Pro Broadcasting

I TOOK THE ATTITUDE OF eliminating what I couldn't control when I was traded. I had pinned all my hopes on my pro football career with the Cleveland Browns, and then I got traded to the Green Bay Packers. All at once, I realized that I could either stand around and worry about what could have been in Cleveland, or I could go ahead and make it all it could be in Green Bay. Suddenly, by eliminating what I couldn't control versus what I could, I found myself in complete control of my career in Green Bay, and I never looked back.

Where I really learned to appreciate dealing with things inside and outside of my control was when I entered into the beverage business in Los Angeles. Two months after I retired from football, I found myself dealing with competition in a way where I said, "I can control how good I can be. I cannot control exactly what the competition does, but I can control how much they impact me."

I set out to identify the fundamental ideas that would ultimately impact my company. In other words, if we had good distribution, if we had our products better displayed, if we had good relationships with the retailers, all of these were things we could control, and ultimately they would help us control our destiny. I could not control what the competition charged for its product, I could not control a lot of things they did, but I could absolutely decide what we could do, and ultimately that would really determine how much impact they had on us.

My mentor, Fred Haviland, executive vice president of Schlitz, said to me, "Willie, as an entrepreneur, you're going to find a lot of tough moments. There are some things you need to learn real quick. One of them is to control what you can control. Do not focus on those things you can't control because they create frustration and they create anxieties that can often lead you to worse results than you would have if you just focus on those things you can control."

I accepted that as good information, and I thought about what Vince Lombardi used to preach to us at Green Bay. He said, "We're going to control what the other team does by controlling what we do. And at the end of the day, we're going to do what we do so well, they won't be able to handle us."

One of the things I say to our radio on-air personalities is "We cannot determine what the other radio stations tend to do. But we can control how good we are." I simply ask them for one thing: "Give me the best four hours of your day when you're on the air. That is the greatest certainty we have of being in control and being competitive." I have found that this really works. Right now our strategy is to superserve the community, superserve our audience, and put ourselves in control. We have elicited their loyalty and their following, and they have developed a commitment to us.

"When I was growing up in Texarkana, I never envisioned that someday I would be an individual who had owned several companies, served on the board of fifteen publicly traded companies, and done things I could have never imagined, including being inducted into the NFL Hall of Fame.

"Do you have total control of that? No. But you do have a certain amount of control. You play every game with every ounce of energy, every ounce of intelligence, every ounce of desire, and somewhere along the line it just seems as if you've controlled those things that got you there."

—WILLIE DAVIS

"Control isn't really about doing it all. It's about being focused on what you want and pursuing your major goals—not every goal. Control is about making choices and having the courage to let certain things go."

—DR. JOYCE BROTHERS
Psychologist, author, and speaker

"The successful CEOs are the folks who have figured out that business is all about people. The business issues, the ideas and innovations are outside their boat. What they've figured out is that it is the people who are inside their boat."

—MICHAEL MCNEAL
Vice president of business development,
PureCarbon, Inc.

26

Don't Fear Pulling Up Your Anchor

JACK KEMP

Codirector, Empower America; distinguished fellow,
Competitive Enterprise Institute

I WAS THE CAPTAIN AND QUARTERBACK for the San Diego Chargers in the early 1960s when I dislocated and destroyed the middle finger on my throwing hand. I hit a Jets helmet as I was passing to Lance Alworth and smashed the synovial cap, which holds the fluid. My finger blew up to the size of a tennis ball. After trying to rehab for about a week, I received a call from head coach Sid Gillman. He said, "We're going to put you on injured reserve for one game."

The next Monday morning I got a call from Lou Saban, head coach of the Buffalo Bills. Late Saturday night I had been put on injured reserve, and you can't be recalled off injured reserve if you're put on it twenty-four hours before a game, because they don't want the injured

84

reserve list to be manipulated. If you're put on during the week, then you can be taken back off. But according to the old AFL rules, if you were put on the night before a game, you could be picked up unconditionally.

Coach Gillman didn't think I would be picked up because it would be too late Saturday, but he was mistaken. Lou Saban phoned me at my house in San Diego Monday morning and said, "Congratulations! You're now a Buffalo Bill." I said, "Oh, no, I'm not. I was told by Sid Gillman that I was protected." I went immediately to talk to Sid, and he didn't even know at the time that I'd been picked up. Sid said, "Don't worry. I'll take care of it."

Well, twenty-four hours went by, forty-eight hours went by, then seventy-two hours. I found out he couldn't take care of it because I had been sold for the $100 waiver price to the Buffalo Bills, who needed a quarterback. So I said, "I'm going to retire." I told Ralph Wilson, the owner of the Bills, that I wasn't going to come to Buffalo, I wasn't going to leave San Diego unless he renegotiated my contract.

I had a new business I'd started in San Diego, Joanne and I had a beautiful home there, and we had two children. I was the first quarterback of the Chargers. I was working for Herb Klein and Jack Murphy at the *San Diego Union*. I said, "I'm not going to go to Buffalo unless you renegotiate my contract and give me what Billy Cannon is making and a 'no-cut clause.'" Ralph turned me down and called my bluff.

I had nothing to do with any of this, other than getting hurt and trying to bluff the Bills. All these other things were going on outside any control that I could possibly have. They were really "outside my boat." Then, after I had been sitting around moping and whining for a couple of weeks, my mother called. She was a very strong person. My dad was a small businessman, and my mother was "the matriarch." She said, "Jack, don't you know that no door closes in your life that another door won't be opened? Why don't you recognize that this was meant to be? I believe Buffalo will be an open door for something much better." She was so right.

Joanne and I went to Buffalo, and *wow*! We won two championships. I served in Congress for eighteen years, was secretary of housing for George Bush, and ran for vice president of the United States. All of this happened after I realized I had no control over what was outside my boat. I just had to find a different ocean to unfurl my sail in.

Take a Beach Break

HERB KLEIN

Former director of communications for President
Richard Nixon; now vice president and editor in
chief, Copley Newspapers

I T'S MY BELIEF THAT ON ELECTION DAY, the candidate for
office finds a frustration greater than any time during
the campaign. It's a time when he's not able to do anything about who will win the election and there's not
much he can do to amuse himself. That day is truly outside his boat.

In 1960, Richard Nixon finished his presidential
campaign, and after he got up on the day of the election
and voted in Whittier, he decided to take off. He and Bill
Rogers, who was attorney general for the Eisenhower
administration and later the secretary of state, slipped
away to Laguna Beach. They each bought a pair of
swimming trunks and went walking on the beach,
where they found some Marines playing football. They

joined the game. The Marines had no idea who they were playing with, and there's no record as to who won.

I always envisioned the surprise at the Marine barracks that night when those Marines turned on their television set. Can you imagine the conversation? "Is that who I think it is?" "No, it can't be." "He wasn't a very good quarterback, but is that who I think he is?" "Is that the guy I knocked down?" "I didn't knock him down, did I?" "Yes." "Oh, that's great."

"Part of the theory I have is that you have to try anything and try very hard, but finally there comes a time when there's nothing more you can do. Then you know that you can fall out of the boat with the satisfaction of whatever is going to happen is going to happen. As I've gone through life, it's become more and more an important thing for me to learn."

—HERB KLEIN

**WORRYING
IS REHEARSING
FOR FAILURE.**

27

Rebuild Your Boat

DR. CHARLES EDWARDS
Former president and CEO, Scripps Clinic and
Research Foundation

I N THE FALL OF 1969, we were living just outside
Chicago and I was senior vice president of Booz Allen
& Hamilton, in charge of all its health- and science-
related activities around the world. One day I got a call
from the Nixon administration, and they said, "We want
to see you." I was a Republican and I was more than
casually interested in politics, so I went to Washington.
Bob Finch was the secretary of health, education and
welfare (HEW), and we met with his group at the White
House. They said, "We want you to take over the Food
and Drug Administration."

I was a physician, so naturally I knew of the FDA,
but I didn't know diddly-squat in terms of any of the
details. I said, "Okay, let me have an office and a telephone for three or four hours. I want to talk to some
people who know something about it." We met again

later in the afternoon, and I said, "Yes, I'll take it. But I really need to get brought up to date on certain things." We decided I would go to Washington for about six weeks, have an office in HEW, and get a feel for the FDA and what I wanted to change. Then we'd pull the chain on the commissioner, Herb Ley, and I would take over.

I started to commute from Chicago to Washington. I'd literally been in my office only two days when I got another call late in the afternoon from Bob Finch. He said, "Come on over. I've got to talk to you." Washington's afternoon newspaper at that time, *The Star*, had come out with a headline that read, "LEY FIRED, EDWARDS NEW COMMISSIONER." Someone had leaked the story that I was going to take his place. Finch told me, "I just talked to Herb Ley, and he has resigned." He added, "It's all yours, fella."

Talk about "outside my boat." I didn't even know where the FDA was. I said to Bob, "I've got to use your car and driver." I arrived at the headquarters of the FDA and immediately went up to the commissioner's office. I walked in and said to his administrative assistant, "I'm Dr. Edwards, here to see Dr. Ley." I'll never forget that moment. She looked at me as if to say, "You miserable son of a bitch, what are you doing here?"

I'd never met Ley in my life, and needless to say, his reception was cold. He had an enormous office, and in this enormous office he had an enormous conference table. It really was gigantic. On this conference table, about every six inches, were piles of papers. I asked him, "What are your main problems?" He looked at the table, pointed to the stacks of paper, and replied, "There they are." There must have been fifty of these piles. He was holding a little plastic football. He tossed it to me and, mixing his metaphors, said, "The ball's in your court," and he walked out the door.

Now I was standing there alone. I didn't know one soul in the FDA. I went out to his administrative assistant and asked, "What are your plans?" She said, "I'm leaving, too." I said, "Please wait. For the sake of the FDA, you can't leave right now. You've got to stay." She said, "All right, I'll stay with you for one month." Her name was Beulah Sink. She stayed with me for my seven years in government, and she was one of the really great women of the world. She suggested I call the head of the Baltimore office of the FDA, who had just completed an organizational study. He came down that evening, and that's the way I got started.

It was not smooth sailing at first because everything was truly outside my boat. So I rebuilt my boat and brought what I needed on board, and everything worked really well. It's generally recognized that ours was one of the best administrations the FDA has ever had. The moral of the story is that just because something starts outside your boat, it doesn't mean it has to stay there.

———————

Rely On Your Network

BEN HADDAD

Former chief of staff for Congressman Bill Lowery;
now senior vice president of communications,
Science Applications International Corporation

O NE OF THE MOST EXCITING TIMES of my life was when I was a legislative assistant for U.S. Congressman Bill Lowery in Washington, D.C. The responsibility of Congress is so vast, it includes everything—foreign affairs, health policy, education—there's not anything it doesn't touch. But you have to understand, and it takes you a while to figure it out, that you, personally, are not responsible for all this stuff. You need to stop worrying that you don't know everything about every subject that appears in the *Congressional Quarterly*, the national journals, or the *New York Times*.

It's frustrating at first. You find yourself working seven-day weeks and at all hours. There is no time off, because you feel as if you can't keep up. At some point you have to realize that that is not your job and it's out of your control. You cannot possibly keep up. You have to let it go.

I don't know when it occurred to me exactly, because we were working ridiculous hours and trying to learn everything. I had judiciary and space and education and a whole bunch of other things in my area of responsibility. However, once you start to interact with some of the experts in each field, you realize they spend their entire lives working on just one little piece of what you're supposed to be learning, and you will never, ever know what they know. So you begin to let go a little bit and say, "You know what? My job is to know where to get the answer. It's not to know the answer."

You start developing a network of people you can phone, because in those days there was no e-mail. You could call somebody who knew everything about a particular educational program dealing with disabled kids. You could tap into the person who handled Russia or the expert who knew the nuclear weapons programs.

Another example was when we were dealing with AWACS on whether we should sell a certain plane to Saudi Arabia. You needed to know who to call on the Israeli side of the issue and who to call on the Arab side of the issue. As long as you could call and get the information and then present it to your congressman in a way that he could make a decision, that's what you needed to do. You didn't have to be the expert on AWACS.

Going in, I don't think you really grasp what your role is. You're so totally overwhelmed. You get frustrated in a hurry because you're just never going to be that omniscient person you aspire to be. But with a little seasoning, you begin to understand the ways of Washington and you become much more effective. You pick your fights, you specialize, and then you let everything else go to your network. It's something you learn from doing, from being there. You build your network inside your boat, and at the same time you make sure you know how to connect with all of the things that are going on outside your boat. The key to your network is your Rolodex. That really is your boat. And I'll tell you what, if you don't have your Rolodex, you'll drown.

"Most of the time, what people spend their time worrying and being upset about is outside their sphere of control. The more you can focus on what's inside your sphere of control, the bigger your sphere will get."

—MICHAEL MCNEAL
Vice president of business development,
PureCarbon, Inc.

"If you only have one problem you're thinking about, it will tend to eat you up. But if you have ten problems, you tend to blow them off and accomplish what you can for the day."

—JIM RIORDAN
Publisher, Seven Locks Press

BE ALERT WHEN SAILING IN UNCHARTED WATERS.

Trust Your Crew

ALICE HAYES
President, University of San Diego

I MANAGE A NUMBER OF AREAS where I have no personal
expertise whatsoever. I first discovered this when I
became executive vice president at St. Louis University.
The newspaper called to interview me, and they found
out I was a biologist and a professor and a university
administrator. They asked me, "How can you run St. Louis
University Hospital, Parks College of Aviation and
Aerospace with its twenty-five airplanes, and a law
school?" I explained to them that in fact I would never
be allowed to do surgery or fly the planes or try a case
in court. They were outside my boat. That was not how
I saw my role as an administrator. My role was not to
perform the functions of all of these initiatives but to
provide oversight, leadership, vision, and guidance.
And that's true here at USD now, as the president.

My heavens, I'm responsible for everything, but I
don't do everything. I am not constructing the Joan Kroc

Institute by myself, nor did I build the Jenny Craig Pavilion. A leader needs to let go and recognize that the people with expertise in specific areas are the ones on whom you should depend to form your policy decisions. I don't feel the need to personally manage everything that goes on within this university. I see my job as working with the people who have those skills. In one sense, they have their own boats but I manage the marina.

I have some personal sanity rules. For example, I don't make appointments on Tuesday nights. That night is outside my boat. Now, there's nothing special about Tuesday night. But I have to tell you when I first said that, they started to think, "What is she doing?" Then they decided since there was no sign of flurry in or out of my house on Tuesday night that it must be because of some television show. Of course there's nothing I'm particularly addicted to on Tuesday night. I just wanted to say, "I am not at your eternal disposal." I need some time for myself, so I made up that rule. Tuesday nights are outside my boat.

For me, being an academic person, I think the area in which I would most like to intervene is academic affairs. It is very hard for me not to get involved in appointments and things like that. Although I have ultimate responsibility for tenure, promotion, hiring, and firing, most of that is delegated. There are temptations in that regard, but you fight them and try to keep them outside your boat.

We have a language in higher education that the business world only recently discovered. We call it "shared governance." We recognize that there are certain areas where some members of the university community have final responsibility. So if you are a member of the board of trustees, you would not ordinarily find yourself involved in faculty appointments or promotions or the content of the curriculum. If you are a faculty member, your responsibility is academic; you don't have the decision about what the schedule for housekeeping should be or the details of administration of financial affairs. In other words, everyone has his or her own boat for which he or she is responsible. People understand their areas, and although we're all tempted to meddle some of the time, we recognize what is inside and what is outside our boat.

It's also a way of respecting competence and recognizing that the more eyes you have looking at some things, the better the result will be. If one person makes all the decisions, even if that person is very good and makes excellent decisions, those decisions will reflect only one perspective. Whereas if you involve more people with different perspectives, the chances are that you'll have better decisions and better results.

———————————

"In the corporate world it's not unusual to be in several boats. The secret is to make a conscientious effort to hire good people. If I have good division heads, boat captains so to speak, and I have clear and concise goals and objectives, I don't have to micromanage. I let them run with it."

—MATT SHEVLIN
Former CFO, CIO, and executive vice president,
AVCO

"Early on, I felt I needed to know everything that was going on. But now I realize I don't have to and that what you can achieve as a team is truly powerful."

—RICHARD POWELL
CEO, Fuxito Worldwide

Cherish What Is Inside Your Boat

DEBI ROLFING
State of Hawaii foster parent

M Y LIFE WAS SO FULL, yet so empty. My days had been richly colored with a very successful career in real estate development and sports marketing with my husband, Mark. But somewhere in my heart of hearts, there was a dream unrealized, a prayer unanswered, because having my own child would forever be outside my boat.

Then life took an enchanting turn. We were approached to become Hawaii State foster parents, and our lives would never be the same again.

It was a beautiful Saturday morning at Kapalua, just before Mother's Day, and it had the makings of great beach weather. But a tinge of sadness crept into my heart. Tomorrow would be Mother's Day . . . and no babies. I shared my feelings with Mark that morning. I barely had the words out of my mouth when the telephone rang. Could we come to Honolulu on Mother's Day to pick up a newborn baby boy? We would need to meet with the birth mother. Getting to know us would help put her mind at ease during this difficult time of being separated from her baby on Mother's Day.

I began to prepare for the baby's arrival. No more time for a heavy heart and melancholy thoughts. The day was spent preparing the nursery, shopping for diapers and formula, and replenishing supplies.

Sunday morning Mark and I flew to Oahu with more luggage carry-ons than we had ever taken on any of our travels to the mainland. Moses basket, car seat, diaper bag, camera bag, leis, gifts. We arrived at Kapiolani Women's and Children's Hospital just after lunch. Finding our way to the nursery, we entered the birth mother's room and introduced ourselves.

The following three hours were at times happy, gut-wrenching, sad, and richly blessed. The teary birth mother prepared for the placement of her newborn son in our care and, more important, to offer another family that precious gift.

We flew home to Maui with a bright-eyed baby boy. We named him after Mark's late father, Jim. So while he was in our care, he was affectionately called "Kimo," the Hawaiian name for James. Throughout the next two weeks, this precious boy with sparkling dark eyes and a head of curls filled every inch of our home with love and joy.

The adoption placement ceremony was held along the shores of Waikiki Beach with fragrant Hawaiian flowers. We were dressed in our muumuus and haku head leis, and Kimo had his maile leaf haku circling his head of curls. The placement was bittersweet, the birth mother struggling to let go while Kimo's new mom eagerly conveyed her gratitude and joy.

For me, the placement was also about letting go. As a foster mother, I am the baby's mommy until he is placed in his new home. During those treasured days, my life revolves around the needs of the newborn. When I arrive at the placement, I have to start my detachment and step back. When I hear that familiar whimper for food or a clean diaper, I can no longer jump to the baby's needs. My job is done. Now it is time for the birth mother and new mom to take over.

It is so hard to let go, but I understand that real pleasures in life must come with a bit of pain. I left for home with my empty Moses basket and an empty spot in my heart.

Yet I was comforted as I tidied the nursery in preparation for the next "Angel Baby." The weeks following a placement are usually spent in reflection as I edit video footage I collected during the baby's stay that captures the first cry, the first smile, and the first bath. The video serves as a gift to the birth and adoptive families so they also share those treasured "firsts."

Sorting through the photos taken during the baby's stay, I savor the magical days shared with these sweet "Angel Babies." Enlargements are made for their baby books, and a favorite photo finds a prominent place on a baby shelf in the nursery. Having just placed photo number nine on the shelf, I take a breath, hold my heart, and wait for the phone to ring again.

———————————

BE THRILLED WITH WHAT IS INSIDE YOUR BOAT.

Changing Course Has Its Rewards

TOM SHERIDAN
Broadcaster, writer, and stay-at-home dad

WHEN MY WIFE AND I HAD OUR THIRD CHILD, we realized things would have to change. We had been running ourselves ragged with two careers and two children, and we decided that two careers did not divide into three children. So I reluctantly left a job I really liked and became "Mr. Mom."

I had been working for an Internet company, Fans Only. It was a dream job. I was writing a regular sports column. I was doing interviews. I had incredible access to people like Bob Davie, the Notre Dame football coach, and Lute Olson, the Arizona basketball coach, because we were doing their Web sites. I gave all this up to be a stay-at-home dad.

My wife is a doctor who specializes in family medicine. When we were both working full time, we'd have to get four people to sign off if she wanted to do some extra work or stay late at the office. Now she only has to come to me and I won't turn her down. Yet in the beginning there was almost resentment between us. She thought it was great that I was leaving my job, which would free me up, and it was best for the family. I wasn't that sure.

For several months I was very bitter. I was sullen, withdrawn, and kind of moody. I thought I had been forced into the decision, and I felt very powerless at the time. I was wondering if I had done the right thing—getting married and having all these children. I was concerned about the position I had put myself in.

But almost immediately, new opportunities arose. I became host of a weekly radio show, I started writing part-time for the *Union-Tribune* newspaper, and I joined a community television station to do football and basketball play-by-play. This had always been my dream. It was high school, but it was still play-by-play.

Gradually, by throwing my old career outside my boat and letting go of my doubts, I built a new and even better boat for myself. I enriched my life. First and foremost, I got to be with my children, but I also got to do all the other things I had always dreamed of doing. What I found was that the feeling of powerlessness I had first experienced turned into a feeling of empowerment. It became a better situation, and I think the most important aspect of it was that I made my wife and kids happy.

The kids were no longer split among a father, a mother, and a caregiver.

There was never an exact moment when I said, "This day is the watershed where it clicked." But today, two and a half years later, there's no question that my wife and I have a better relationship and we have a stronger family unit. My youngest daughter has never known anybody but me to take care of her, and we are best buddies. My son knows the best of me and the worst of me. I frequently think about how incredibly close I am with my kids. There's no way we would've had this kind of relationship if I had stayed on the same course, if I had been away from home sixty hours a week.

Although my initial feeling was that I'd scuttled any chance I ever had at a career, ironically, my decision to give up the perceived control I had turned into the best thing I could ever have done for my career.

"People always worry about the grass being greener on the other side of the fence. But you should be watering the grass on *your* side of the fence."

—EMMITT SMITH
NFL Dallas Cowboys running back

Hold On to Your Lifeboat of Faith

JUDY EPPLER

Owner, Judy Eppler Chevron Station

M Y BIGGEST LIFE CHANGE was finding myself divorced after twenty-six years of marriage, with three daughters and a ten-year-old son to raise. I had no college education. I was clerking at Sav-on drugs and trying to figure out what in the name of God I was going to do to support myself and my family, and feeling as if I had no control over my life.

I thought, okay, what are my options? I could stay at Sav-on. I knew they liked me and I could probably go into management, but I wasn't really sure I wanted to do that. I could not see myself doing that. My son was an avid baseball player, and I wanted to have time to watch him play.

It was a lot of faith and friends that really interceded for me and gave me a lifeboat. It was a hell of a gamble.

I had to get an SBA loan, and I didn't have any collateral. My brother, who is a priest, quitclaimed our family home, which he and my mother had owned, and gave me the collateral. I went to the SBA and got a loan and purchased the Chevron service station from my ex-husband, then found out the business was just about bankrupt.

It took me two years to climb out of that hole. But the nice thing about it was, it gave me some flexibility. I could go watch my son play baseball. He was a pitcher, and now he's a scout for the Colorado Rockies.

I purchased the Chevron station in 1988. I didn't know a thing about gasoline, just that you put it in your car. I knew nothing about tanks and EPA and all the environmental things. I literally walked in with a feather duster and started front-facing all of the shelves. My daughter Debbie said, "Mom, you've got to come into the office and learn the business." I said, "Not right now; first I'll dust." But then I jumped in with both feet, and the rest is history. I took this station from near bankruptcy to a $5-million-a-year business. We are one of the top thirteen stations in the nation for Chevron, and we've received gold and platinum awards from the company.

Things just happened. There were miracles in my life. It was a true faith walk, because God put people into my life. Once I let go of having to make it happen and feeling the stress; once I climbed into the backseat and let God take over the driving; once I allowed myself to let go and then look for the good in what happened and then follow that good, it brought me more blessings than I could have ever imagined.

What's important is the legacy you leave in this world, the people whose lives you've touched and changed for the better. When kids come to work for me, I say, "God didn't put you on this earth to work at Judy Eppler Chevron; this is a means toward an end. That means you go to college and I'll be in the front row on the day of your graduation." I've launched two of them so far, and I'm ready to launch my third.

This is more to me than a service station business or a gasoline business. This is a walk with my fellowman. This is a life business.

———————————

"I think we are all tempted to try to control everything related to our lives, but the reality is that we must quite often sit back and let life take its own course."

—LAMAR HUNT
Founder, American Football League

"When it gets so tough and it doesn't seem as if there's a reasonable answer in front of us, it's time to quit trying to control the situation and just let things happen."

—DOUG MANCHESTER
President, Manchester Resorts

**YOU DISCOVER
THE STRENGTH
OF YOUR BOAT
BY HOW IT
RESPONDS IN
A STORM.**

Take Charge of
Your Life

JACKIE TOWNSEND
President, Townsend Agency

I N 1993, I WAS SEEING A PSYCHOLOGIST because of my
divorce. Being Catholic, I was having a lot of guilt
feelings about going through a divorce after eighteen
years of marriage, and at the same time, I was having a
large disagreement with my ex-employer. I felt I was the
massive failure of all time, when my psychologist asked
me a very important question. He said, "What would
you like to do?" I said, "You know, I'd really like to start
my own business so I can show that you can treat
people with respect, help them work on their strengths
and, at the same time, make the business a success. I
really want to prove to myself that you can be successful by treating people with respect." He said, "Well,
why don't you do it?" It was that simple. I said, "Do you

think I can?" He said, "You're the most capable person I know. I think you can do it if you decide that's what you want to do."

I walked out of his office, and I decided right then that I was going to take charge of my life. I was not going to give the reins to anyone else ever again. Within one month the Townsend Agency was up and running. We're an integrated marketing firm that does advertising, public relations, and strategic marketing for new-economy businesses.

In the beginning, because I had no money, I cleaned the toilets, vacuumed the floors, answered the phone, wrote the new business proposals, and did all the work. The first thing I gave up when we had a little success was the janitor's job. Everything just happened. I had clients before I opened the door. One person asked me, "What makes you think you're going to succeed?" I said, "Because I can't afford to fail. I'm a single mom with two kids and no child support payments and nobody's going to take care of them."

The business is doing phenomenally well. We did about $7 million last year. We have a great group of people. The whole culture here is based on the way I want to live my life, because I choose to do it that way. It took me years to realize that you can choose to be in relationships or you can choose not to be. That was a powerful lesson. Since then I have learned a lot about what's not in my boat. I'm still learning that with my boys.

They are now twenty-two and twenty-four, and letting go of children, particularly when you raise them as a single mom, is very difficult. But a huge part of letting go happened when I finally realized it wasn't in my boat, so why was I putting so much energy into it? Why didn't I put the energy into what I could control?

In essence, you must let go of the things that are out of your control and control the things that you are in control of 100 percent. It requires accepting complete responsibility for your part in what you do. It's very easy to blame other people. It took me a long time to learn this, but once you figure it out, it's very freeing. Life is so much more fun because you choose to be in relationships, you choose to work on people's strengths, and you choose to eliminate obstacles.

If you focus on what you have control over, all of a sudden you can make that better, because you do have control. It's so empowering. Too many people sit around whining and moaning. When you do that, you're really giving your power away to somebody else.

If you're truly powerless in a situation, maybe you need to be somewhere else. But if you recapture your power, then all of a sudden the upside is so freeing. Now when you look in the mirror in the morning, you see who is truly responsible for how your day's going to go.

———————

Find New Strength
by Letting Go

SUNNIVA SORBY

Explorer, writer, educator, and motivational speaker

O N JANUARY 14, 1993, at approximately 6:05 P.M.
(EST), we made history as the first women's team
to reach the South Pole without the aid of sled dogs or
motorized vehicles. The four of us skied seven hundred
miles in sixty-seven days, each pulling two-hundred-
pound sleds and battling temperatures as cold as minus
50 degrees F. and winds up to a hundred miles per hour.
We were part of the American Women's Trans-Antarctic
Expedition.

In addition to accomplishing a first for women, we
were doing research to further understand what happens
to the female body when subjected to such cold conditions for a long period of time. What happens to the
menstrual cycle? What happens when you're eating
6,000 calories a day and you're pulling a heavy sled? At

another level, what happens to the mind when you have a goal but it's so far away you can't see it? How does the level of motivation and the commitment to that goal change from day to day, and how does that impact the whole team aspect?

In anything we do, we have a perception of ourselves, certainly of our strengths and not as frequently of our weaknesses. We like to dwell on our strengths. Going into this project, I was the youngest of the four team members and I truly felt I was the fittest. I knew that wasn't going to be the single most important element; I knew the mental aspect was a key factor, as was the spiritual, but I never thought my body would fail me. But it did.

Six weeks into the sixty-seven-day expedition I became very, very sick with bronchitis and tendinitis, which meant I couldn't do two of the things that were required of me: walk and breathe. Because of that I was very weak and was forced to travel in a lot of pain. I felt I wasn't contributing to the big picture. I wasn't even contributing individually.

I didn't tell anybody. I tried so hard to control how I moved. Everything in me was crumbling. The more I fought it, the more I tried to control it, the more it crumbled. My story revolves around the transformation that happened in the span of a few days. I completely let go of control over myself and trusted that help was going to come in the form of my three teammates. It was simply letting go. In doing so you start opening yourself up to seeing things differently. There's a wonderful quote by the great French novelist Marcel Proust: "Perhaps the real voyage of discovery consists not in seeking new landscapes, but in having new eyes."

It was a very poignant time in my life, and I think a lot of people can relate to it because we all try so hard to control our image. My image was young, strong, healthy, I can do anything. Maybe it's borderline naive to feel as if nothing will ever happen to you, but my spirit has always carried me through the down times. I realized that this was my single greatest strength. Letting go of the image of oneself to allow change to happen and thus allow what you perceive to be a weakness emerge as a strength was probably the greatest gift I could have given myself.

When I let go, I did the only thing I knew how to do, and that was cry. I sobbed in the comfort of the vast white Antarctic landscape. As daunting as that might seem to a lot of people, I felt so comfortable out there because nobody was watching. I had these big glacier glasses on that have side shields, so my three teammates couldn't tell that I was crying. I just sobbed.

I don't usually let myself cry. I'm Norwegian-born, sort of the stoic Viking personality. Don't show emotion; that's a sign of weakness. But I just let it go. The reason I let it go was that I had been fighting so hard to control the pain and to control my emotions that when I finally did relinquish control, the emotions came flooding forward. That was the first step.

After that, I was in a place of peacefulness where I realized this trip was not about me. For a while, because of the pain, I had focused too much on Sunniva Sorby. When I reinforced my knowledge that the trip was more about Ann Bancroft, Anne Dal Vera, Sue Giller, and Sunniva Sorby, the four of us, it was then up to me to be honest with them about how I was and what kind of help I needed. Oddly enough, when I told them, it created a much stronger team component, and it actually turned out to be the thing that kept the four of us together for that long, lonely crossing.

Throughout the whole trip I was sick. Two years later I found out that the expedition leader, Ann Bancroft, had been so concerned about me that she thought I might slip away in the night because I was so sick with that bronchial infection. But I made it to the South Pole, and on some level I was stronger when I came back because I had a different perception of what strength was.

Strength has everything to do with one's spirit, one's ability to get out of one's own world for the sake and for the goodness of others. That is real strength. I used to think that by asking for help you were weak. I was taught that growing up. I went into this project with that mentality, but I learned you can't survive in any scenario without a community.

When I got out of my own way and I let go of my own desire and willingness to control myself, when I let go of all that, I built a community of strength around me with my teammates. To me, that was unbelievable. The lightbulb went on. When I came home, I got it. I understood. But it took this expedition experience for me to understand. Now when somebody asks for help, I see that as a real sign of strength.

"I have that desire to want to always see what's possible."

—SUNNIVA SORBY

"You can go as far as you want in anything."

—SALLY JONES
Director, ACE Parking

36

Control How
You Respond

SUZYN WALDMAN

New York Yankees television announcer

Y OUR FIRST INSTINCT when you find you have breast cancer is to say, "All right, get it out of me, tell me what I need to do to get on with my life." That's something that you just do. But how do you get on with your life? I didn't think I had a choice. But even when the whole thing is outside your boat, you still have a choice. You can either go on or you can give up and die, in this case literally. When given the choice, people will always look at this and say, "Okay, what do I do to go on?" My first thought was not to tell anybody, but obviously I had to. Then I found out that people wanted me to go away because I had breast cancer. Everyone was very nice, but it was almost as if I was starting over in sports broadcasting. It was, "Yes, dear. When you get better, come back and we'll talk about it."

I was diagnosed three weeks before spring training. That was the first year I was going to have a full-time job as a New York Yankees announcer. I'd worked fifteen years for that. I thought to myself, I can't go away and come back when I'm better. Somebody else will be sitting in my seat.

There's a great saying, "You can't control the wind, but you can control your sails." I thought of that a lot, because breast cancer was nothing I had asked for. I had no control over it; it was totally outside my boat. But what I discovered was, people didn't want me around because I was sick. I didn't feel sick, I didn't look sick, but I was sick. And something else kicked in. I wasn't going to let it beat me. I continued to work and I probably shouldn't have, but I did. It kept me going, it kept me alive.

I remember calling George Steinbrenner on the phone when they were futzing around with my contract. I said, "George, it's Suzyn. Are you not going to give me this job because I have breast cancer?" Just like that. And he said, "What the hell are you talking about?"

I fired my first oncologist because he wouldn't let me go to spring training. I said to the hospital, "You'd better find me somebody, because I'm going to spring training and unless you want me to die, you'd better find a way to do this." They sent me to a supposedly overaggressive female doctor. She was just great with me. She said, "We'll work it out. We'll do this because quality of life is very important when you're fighting this kind of thing."

I missed very few games. I missed the day I had chemo, once every three weeks for six months, and I missed the day after because I was so sick. Other than that, I gave myself shots on the plane. The Yankees were awesome. I mean, it came out of nowhere. I never would have expected this, but George and the trainers set up doctors for me all over the country, wherever we were, so that I could have my blood tests every few days to make sure I wasn't going to die. I had Neupogen shots to keep my white blood cell count up. They were refrigerated in every clubhouse in the American League, wherever we were. I took them for ten days after every chemo treatment. It was amazing.

I found such a network of people whom I thought I had only covered professionally and in whose face I had merely stuck a microphone. The guys on the Yankees were great. I traveled with the team; if I started getting nauseous, all of a sudden I'd turn around and there would be some player standing next to me with club soda. It was incredible. I never said a word. I lost my hair, my eyebrows, my eyelashes, everything. I wore a wig and makeup on television.

The greatest thing is, I know I helped other people. I received hundreds and hundreds of letters during that time. I got one from a woman who had stage four breast cancer. This was in 1996. She said, "I just want to thank you, because my husband had brought home two tickets to the World Series to see my team, the Yankees, and I wouldn't go because I have no hair and I had a crisis. If it hadn't been for you, I would have missed seeing my team in the World Series because I was saying, 'I can't go, I can't go.' Then I turned on the television, and there you were. I looked at the screen and I said, "If she can do it, I can do it." I put a scarf on my head, and I went and saw the Yankees win."

My television partner, Bobby Mercer, never even knew I had a wig on. He had no idea. He just knew that I was throwing up all over the place. My mother told me I never looked so good as when I had that wig on. It wasn't easy; it was horrible. But what comes out of something you can't control is something you can control. You can't control what happens to you but you can control what you do with it.

There's so much that goes with being a breast cancer survivor because there's no cure, so it's in the back of your mind every day. It has been five years, and every time I get an ache I think, Oh God, it's back. It doesn't go away. But you learn to live with it, and you learn to help other people. It begets other things.

When Darryl Strawberry was diagnosed with cancer, I was there for Darryl. Darryl was there for Joe Torre. Joe was there for Mel Stottlemyre. It just keeps going. You can control what you do with it. You're supposed to give something back in this life. Cancer isn't what I would have chosen, and I'm sure it isn't what Joe Torre would have chosen either, but you deal with it.

"When I started auditioning on Broadway, I wanted to be Mary Martin. That's all I wanted to be. But I wasn't blond and cute. Mary Martin was outside my boat. I said to the producer, 'I thought theater was the art of illusion,' and he said, 'Well, maybe it is, but not in this cast of *Sound of Music*.'"

—SUZYN WALDMAN

**THE MEASURE
OF A PERSON IS NOT
WHAT HE DOES
WHEN HE'S STANDING
ON TOP OF THE WORLD
BUT WHAT HE DOES
WHEN HE'S STANDING
ON THE DECK AND HIS
SHIP IS SINKING.**

37

Reevaluate Your Life

DUNCAN HANNAY

Manager, Strategic Alliances, E*Trade Canada

I T WAS IN FEBRUARY OF 1996 I was thirty-three years old and happily married. We had two children and a third on the way. My wife was nine months pregnant, and I was fairly successful in my career. I was vice president of marketing at an engineering firm, and life was basically good.

It was just one of those things that hits you out of the blue. I was happy and healthy. I had a short bout with what we believed to be a strep throat virus. I struggled with it a little bit, but after a week or so of being under the weather, I slowly got better.

It began with a droopy eyelid. I remember the day. The weather was mild for Toronto in February; there was no snow on the ground. I washed both cars and raked the entire yard. I did a lot of physical activities, but all through the day I had an eyelid that was half shut. That evening I was feeling a little bit tired, and my wife insisted that I go into Emergency to get my droopy eyelid checked out. The doctor on call dismissed it as potentially a little bit of facial palsy. He told me I would be fine, just to go home and monitor the situation, but I needn't worry.

I went home and went to bed. I woke up around four in the morning, feeling unusual. As I got out of bed, I fell flat on the floor. My legs weren't functioning, and paralysis had begun to set in, but I was still able to get back up on my feet and, with assistance, ambulate my way downstairs to the kitchen table. My wife called her father, and the two of us went back to Emergency.

I was put into an observation room and left there. Finally I got frustrated that I wasn't getting the attention I thought I deserved, so I got up and now I couldn't walk at all. I crawled up the hallway to the nursing station. By this time, I was getting weaker and weaker and my arms were beginning to become useless and I couldn't stand. They immediately called in a neurologist, and a few hours later they diagnosed me with GBS, Guillain-Barré syndrome.

GBS is essentially an inflammatory disorder of the peripheral nerves, so it has nothing to do with your brain or your central nervous system, but rather the peripheral nerves that serve your muscles at your extremities. It comes in varying severities. They actually don't really know what causes it, but in roughly 50 percent of the cases it's preceded by some kind of a viral infection. The theory is that one's own antibodies turn on one's own tissue. So it's basically your own system turning on itself and consuming your peripheral nervous system.

In my case it was very bad. Some people will get it and experience a little bit of weakness in their legs or arms and recover fully within a couple of weeks. Seventy percent recover fully within six months. But I, unfortunately, was in the percentile of people who have it quite severely, and it affected my entire body, including my ability to breathe.

Within twenty-four hours I was completely paralyzed from head to toe. I was put on a respirator because I was no longer able to breathe on my own. I was literally encased in my own body with no normal bodily functions and completely dependent upon mechanical ventilation for breathing. Also, I was in excruciating pain, which is not uncommon in severe cases of GBS, because every nerve in the body is being simultaneously consumed by the condition.

I lost sixty pounds. I was just skin and bones with no bodily functions when I was finally able to open my eyes. I had intense pain and could communicate only by blinking my eyes. Fortunately, I had an extremely supportive wife and family. If I had to point to anything in terms of my ability to recover without going completely insane, I'm sure it was due to them. I gained strength through my wife and the rest of my family and her family, and they offered tremendous support both to her and to me throughout the process.

I was in the hospital for thirteen months and went from being a complete quadriplegic, ventilator-dependent, to slowly rebuilding. By the time I got out of the hospital, I was still unable to feed myself or even hold a pen or ambulate independently. I was able to move about a little bit with two forearm crutches. It was a challenging time because I still needed a lot of help, from daily bathing and dressing to eating.

I spent another two years rehabbing myself and through the people whom I had worked with I obtained a voice-activated computer, because I couldn't type or work a mouse. Toward the end of my stay in the hospital I started working on my voice-activated computer, and that really helped me to maintain my sanity and to stay in touch with the outside world.

I developed quite a passion for the Internet and set myself up with a little home office. I spent a lot of time researching and learning more about the Web, and I even traded some stock on-line, which is eventually where I ended up in my career.

I think it was Hippocrates who said that healing is a matter of time, but it's sometimes a matter of opportunity. I took a lot of time during my rehabilitation to reexamine my life. When you're encased in your body, completely paralyzed on a ventilator, looking out at the world, it gives you a slightly different perspective on things, such as what's really important in life. Clearly, what is important is my wife and my family and the people around me.

What car I drive and how much money I have seem completely unnecessary and immaterial. So in a strange way, it gives you the opportunity to refocus and reevaluate your life. I spent those couple of years while I was rehabbing doing just that.

What I realized was that certainly there are things that are outside your boat; there is no point in spending a whole lot of time worrying about those. And I really didn't. I knew I would get progressively better, and I viewed that more as a challenge. I constantly tested myself and set goals about improving. I knew I couldn't control the things outside my boat, but there was enough in my boat that I could use to get better and to reevaluate my career, my family, and my situation in life.

It's been a life-changing process but one that I'm better off for. Even though I still don't walk terribly well—I wear leg braces from the knees down—and I have limited hand function and certain physical disabilities and there are things I'll never do again, I actually feel better off for it.

My wife and I have a better, stronger relationship than we've ever had. We have a wonderful family and a very loving environment. On the professional side, I'm much more satisfied in what I'm doing now than what I was doing before. I wasn't particularly unhappy then, but at the same time, I wasn't terribly fulfilled. I took the opportunity to move on to something different. I'm now much happier doing what I'm doing. Our family has a much better lifestyle and certainly a more balanced lifestyle as a result of what happened.

"Never ask yourself why, but ask yourself what. Don't ask yourself, 'Why me? Why did this happen?' Instead, ask yourself, 'What can I do to be a better person as a result of it? What can I do to get better and what can I focus on to make a better life for me and my family?' "

—Nurse Sister Margaret's advice to Duncan Hannay during his thirteen months in the hospital recovering from Guillain-Barré syndrome

38

Be True to Yourself

WILLIAM RAY
Software sales executive, IBM

I'M REALLY A PRODUCT of the civil rights movement. I was born in 1954, and that was the year of *Brown v. Board of Education,* the Supreme Court decision that declared racial segregation in public schools unconstitutional.

I grew up in Asheville, North Carolina, a small town in the South, and I remember the beginnings of the civil rights movement in which my older brother and sister participated in marches and sit-ins. My father was a businessman who operated a funeral home, and I remember that across the street from his business was a gas station with white and colored bathrooms. At the square in the center of town the water fountains were labeled "White" and "Colored."

My father was fairly prominent in town in terms of taking a leadership role in the black community. He participated in the Human Relations Council. When my father realized the schools in Asheville were going to be integrated, he asked that I be a part of the first group. There were six of us, and we entered the second grade in 1960. We were part of that first wave.

The first day I went to school, I was in the bathroom when I got mugged by a bully who called me a bunch of names, including the "N" word, and took my lunch money. When I got home after school with my bumps and bruises—I never will forget this—my mother sat me down and said, "Always remember that people who don't know your name will call you different names."

At that time I understood what was happening around me. Sure, I was only six years old and small, but the visible signs of discrimination were right in front of me with the bathrooms and water fountains and having to sit upstairs at the movies. So even though I was small, I understood there was change going on. I was right in the middle of this environment, it was a little bit dangerous, and certainly getting beat up was a rude awakening in the beginning.

My older sister told me, "People will call you names, but they don't know your intellect, they don't know your character, they don't know that you're a good person. They're simply looking at you for the color of your skin, not for who you are. You need to view them as ignorant people. They don't understand. The way to fight back at ignorant people is not with your fists but with your mind. If you can outperform them, then they will accept you in the end."

Four years later, in the sixth grade, I was elected president of the student body, which was 95 percent white. Although it took a few years, just as my sister told me, goodness and hard work made a difference. I think that's the real measure of the story. If you're true to yourself and you work hard, in time that will overcome prejudice and mistrust.

"The issue is, how do you accept a challenge and how do you rebound from a challenge? You're not going to win every deal. If you let the ones you lose get you down, you won't be ready for the next opportunity coming down the road."

—WILLIAM RAY

"Sometimes what you think is the worst thing that could happen to you ends up being the best thing that could happen to you."

—JESSE RAY
William Ray's father

39

Row Your Boat

TOM WORNHAM

Senior vice president and regional manager,
Wells Fargo Bank

T HE LARGEST OUT-OF-MY-BOAT CHALLENGE, lifewise, was my dad's problems when I was growing up. He went to prison, and I went from being a rich kid to a poor kid.

Dad had made his first million at age thirty-six. He was a bright guy, the son of a three-star general. Everything was great, and then he started *Oceans Magazine*. It ended up being a complete failure. We lost everything we had. The house was auctioned off the courthouse steps; the cars were repossessed. Mom and I ended up moving to a little bungalow. My folks had gone from donating the swimming pool at Bishop's School to my mom becoming its receptionist. Thankfully there was a job there.

Investors had put a lot of money into *Oceans Magazine*. The money was lost, and the investors filed for grand theft. Dad spent eighteen months in prison at Chino. I had no idea when my father was going to be paroled. I knew it would happen one day. But we had a life to live.

We drove up to Chino every other Sunday and had lunch with him in the yard. It was a great time to learn, because most of my friends were kids of my parents' friends, and in 1972 it wasn't all that cool to go to jail. I didn't see a lot of people after that for many years. It was a great lesson in finding out who your friends really are.

Dad was paroled on July 4, 1974, and was ultimately pardoned by Governor Jerry Brown. He was put on the Board of Corrections and has spent the last twenty years working with the board in one capacity or another as a consultant.

This happened when I was twelve years old. I didn't have the latitude to get into trouble, so it forced me to walk the straight-and-narrow path. I think that's what drove me to be class president every year and to get into Berkeley.

It was just my mom and me. My older sisters were in college; Wendy was at Stanford, and Cindy was at UC Santa Barbara. It was one of those times when you had to suck it up and say, "I'm not going to give people the satisfaction of writing us off."

I threw 115 newspapers on my paper route the morning my dad's picture was in it with the headline reading, "THOMAS V. WORNHAM GOES TO JAIL." I guarantee you, halfway through the route I was getting more distance than I'd ever gotten before as the adrenaline kicked in.

That's when I decided I had two options. One was to roll over and play dead, and the other was to get through this. And we did. My mom is a trouper and continues to be. My dad's a trouper. My folks stayed together. This has a happy ending. Wendy went on to Harvard Medical School after finishing Stanford in three years, and Cindy went on to have a successful career.

After I graduated from Berkeley I came back to San Diego with the priority of rebuilding the family name. A by-product of that was becoming the youngest assistant vice president, vice president, regional vice president, and senior vice president Wells Fargo Bank has ever had.

I had to choose a life path because of events outside of my boat. I thought of my dad every day, and he remains my best friend. He's a huge part of my life. But I could not control the time when he was in jail. I could control only my boat; I just had to keep on rowing.

"When you take a good blow to the chin, you can either lie down on the canvas and take your ten count or you can get up and start swinging again."

—JAN SCHULTZ
Former vice president of marketing, Sea World;
president and CEO, Balboa Travel

**THE PAST IS
OUTSIDE YOUR BOAT.**

**NOTHING YOU CAN DO
CAN CHANGE THE PAST.**

**EVERYTHING YOU DO
CHANGES THE FUTURE.**

Sail in Familiar Waters

JACK BLANKINSHIP
Partner, Blankinship & Foster
Personal Financial Advisors

I OPENED MY FINANCIAL PLANNING PRACTICE in 1974, back during the racquetball craze, and my partner and I had an investor who wanted to build a racquetball court. We looked for additional investors, but we couldn't find any. As it turned out, we funded the whole thing ourselves. It was built in Artesia, California, right off the 91 freeway. It was a big, beautiful place, with lots of terrazzo and marble. It had ten courts.

We opened the doors in April 1976, just about the time racquetball was petering out. My pro forma indicated that we needed a 38 percent play rate to break even, and the highest we ever got was 36 percent.

All through that summer I just agonized and agonized, and for about a month I lived in the office of that doggone thing. I remember promising God that if I ever got out of that situation, I would never leave my beloved practice of financial planning.

All of a sudden in October, Wayne Hughes called. Wayne was the owner and builder of Public Storage miniwarehouses. He ended up buying us out, debt and everything.

I came home with my tail between my legs, and I've kept my nose to the grindstone ever since. I've had opportunities to get away from financial planning, but I tell that story every time. That's my story. We got into something in which we had no expertise. It was really outside our boat. We didn't know what was going on. The best thing we did was to abandon ship.

"Sometimes you just have to give up. You can fight and fight, but you can't control that which is outside your boat."

—DOUG MANCHESTER
President, Manchester Resorts

Don't Let Storm Clouds Dampen Your Spirits

JAN SCHULTZ

Former vice president of marketing, SeaWorld;
president and CEO, Balboa Travel

ONE DAY IN THE EARLY 1970s, it dawned on me how many kids in southern California, unless they went to the mountains, had never seen snow. So I had what I thought was a brilliant idea of doing SnowWorld at SeaWorld.

The first thing I wanted to do was build a snow mountain, thirty or forty feet high, that the kids could slide down. We quickly discovered that the construction required to make it safe would be unaffordable. So we found a place in the park that had nice little hills about ten feet high. I must say, I had a lot of doubters. When word got around we were going to do SnowWorld, a lot of folks thought I had lost my mind. Anytime I walked through the park, they'd say, "Hey, there goes that nut who's going to bring in snow."

144

The plan was to hold it the two weeks over the holidays. Opening day was the Saturday before Christmas. I ordered four hundred tons of snow. It actually consisted of huge blocks of ice that they crushed and then blew as snow. As we got closer to opening day, it looked as if there was a good possibility of rain, so I told the operations guys, "Look, we've got to put the snow down the day before, on Friday. I think you ought to get the tarp from Jack Murphy Stadium and bring it over here to cover the snow." They said, "Okay, okay, Mr. Schultz," just humoring me.

At about 3 A.M. on the Saturday of our opening, I was awakened by a heavy, heavy rain. I got up, dressed, and hurried to the park. There was no tarp, and my SnowWorld at SeaWorld had turned into SwimWorld. This was certainly something that was outside my boat. It was in the hands of a much bigger man with a much bigger boat.

I called the guy who ran Union Ice and said, "You've got to get over here, we have to create the snow again." I didn't know if it was going to be a success or not, but he came and started to blow the ice. At about 7:30 A.M., I went to the front gate, and there was a line of kids that stretched for almost a half mile. They were in their stocking caps and their mittens, and they had their little sleds. I knew then that we had a winner.

The problem was that SnowWorld was supposed to open at 9 A.M. but there wasn't enough snow. So we made announcements all morning long, Union Ice did its job, and we opened at noon. I have to tell you, I wasn't a very happy camper when I woke up at three that morning, but when I saw the line of kids, I knew it had been worth the effort. We doubled our December attendance, and SnowWorld ran for fifteen straight years. It became a SeaWorld tradition, but it was almost rained out.

———————————

42

When the Wind Shifts, React Quickly

JAN SCHULTZ

Former vice president of marketing, SeaWorld;
president and CEO, Balboa Travel

A FTER MANY YEARS in the theme park industry, I came to Balboa Travel. In the early years before I got here, the travel agency business was very simple. You booked a trip and the agency got 10 percent, and the customer didn't pay anything extra for the service. The same was true with corporate clients. So if you booked a million dollars' worth of travel, the agency would earn $100,000. It was good money.

I entered the business in 1997, and in September of that year the airlines cut commissions from 10 percent to 8 percent on domestic fare tickets, with caps of $25 on one-way tickets and $50 on round-trip tickets. The airlines suddenly made the announcement, it took effect the next day, and overnight our company's income decreased significantly.

In November 1998, the airlines did the same thing with the international commissions. They put a cap of $50 and $100 on tickets. This meant if we booked a $4,000 round-trip ticket to London, instead of earning 10 percent of that, or $400, now all we made was $100. This change cost our company a million dollars in revenue. We simply couldn't afford to take that kind of a hit. In a single day we went from a projected high-six-figure profit to a projected high-six-figure loss. This was something that was definitely outside our boat.

It was tough. I was madder than hell. I was so mad at the airlines I wouldn't even let their representatives into my office. I knew it wasn't their fault; it was their management's decision. I'd never been in a business where vendors had such immediate control over your revenue.

We had to take care of what was inside our boat in a hurry, or we would sink. We couldn't wait. The only way to survive was to change how we operated. I had to let 10 percent of the workforce go. We got lean and mean. We got tougher. In addition, we had to go to our clients, who were not used to writing checks, and say, "Look, you have to start paying for our professional services. You pay your landscaper, you pay your barber, you pay your doctor, you pay everyone else, and now you have to pay us." That was a slow and very difficult process.

Lo and behold, in the next six months we finished the year making our original budget projection. The year finished much stronger than I ever anticipated. We learned a lot. It was a major turn in the future growth of Balboa Travel.

Then in October 1999 the airlines did it again. They cut commissions from 8 percent to 5 percent, another $500,000 loss for us. I was not happy. I was mad. But you know what? We didn't have to lay anybody off; we had a much stronger team in place. We were much more dedicated, we were brighter, we were smarter, and we ended up with a record year after thirty-two years in the travel business.

"You should try to develop a course as straight ahead as possible with what you can control, but there will always be a lot of zigging and zagging."

—JIM BERGLUND
General partner, Enterprise Partners Venture Capital

**THE ART OF
BUSINESS SUCCESS
IS PAYING ATTENTION
TO WHAT IS INSIDE
YOUR BOAT.**

43

Accept That Sometimes You Will Run Aground

JIM BERGLUND

General partner, Enterprise Partners Venture Capital

WHAT'S OUTSIDE YOUR BOAT is when you buy a business and fire the current CEO, and the next guy you hire screws up. Everything about him told you he was good, from all his references to his previous experience—everything—but then he doesn't perform to expectations. You did everything you could to hire the right person, but there's nothing you can do now except start over again.

Because you inherited the first CEO when you invested in the company, it was a little easier to replace him because he wasn't "your guy." But the second one is the one you put into place, and it becomes very difficult to face up to

151

the reality that you screwed up. You realize that this guy has to go and you need to find somebody else.

The same thing could happen all over again. You can't predict what people are going to do. That's the most miserable part. You think you're going to know. You think you know the personality and the background, but once they're placed in the job, they do things differently than you think they should. It's beyond your control. It's outside your boat. You just take your chances and hope that it's going to work out the way you want. But the challenge is always people.

"People are almost always outside your boat, because people aren't predictable in any way, shape or form."

—JIM BERGLUND

"Business, real business, is not numbers and it's not money. It's people. You have to be able to know and to judge people."

—ANDRÉ MEYER
Financier

44

Persevere Through Choppy Seas

BOB RAISSMAN
Columnist, *New York Daily News*

THE AFTERNOON PAPER in Greenville, South Carolina, was the third newspaper I'd worked at. I'd just come off a weekly and this was a daily paper, so it was a big step for me. I was on the news side covering labor unions.

Greenville is a big textile area, and a lot of textile workers were coming down with something called "brown lung disease." I really became involved in writing about it. Meanwhile, the unions were trying to organize, and I got the feeling that although the paper was letting me cover the situation, it was not pleased with what was happening.

One day I was working on that story, and one of the editors came to me and said, "I don't want you to do that today. I want you to do this story on kids." It was around Christmas, and shoes were being donated to

153

needy children. To me, anybody could have done this shoe story; I just wanted to keep pursuing the "brown lung disease" stories. I lost my temper and told the editor I wasn't going to do the kid story, I was going to do my story. About an hour later I was in the managing editor's office, and I was fired.

I packed all my stuff, went back to New York City, moved in with my parents, and started looking for another job in journalism. But I kept getting rejected. I told myself that it wasn't due to the firing because I knew that was outside my control. There was simply an antiunion philosophy at the newspaper, and they weren't comfortable with what I had been writing.

It took almost two years before I was hired at the *Winston-Salem Journal*. It was a matter of persistence. I drove down to North Carolina, met the editor, and kept bugging him, so he finally hired me. If I'd said to myself that I wasn't good enough because I was rejected so often, I wouldn't have been so determined. But I didn't let that one thing stop me. It was outside my boat.

"It's easy to get diverted by all the variables outside your control, to let them eat away at your vision and self-confidence. Detours will doom you. Lose faith in yourself, and you'll fulfill your own worst prophecy."

—BILL PARCELLS
Former NFL head coach

**THE GREATEST
RISK IS NOT
TAKING ONE.**

45

Keep Your Emotions in Check

CRAIG MASBACK
CEO, USA Track & Field

WELCOME TO THE CROWDED SKIES, which in some places is known as a bus service with wings. Air travel is now completely surrounded by the strong possibility of unpleasantness, such as flights canceled, flights delayed, flights delayed and then canceled, flights overbooked, flights late, missed connections, arrive Gate 3 leave Gate 53, mechanical problems, and the ubiquitous lost luggage. This has become a way of life and a cause of high blood pressure for travelers around the world.

I fly thousands of miles worldwide every year, and I have found a way to keep my blood pressure from climbing off the charts. I call it T.W.E., "Travel Without Emotion." It's very similar to T.O.M.B., "That's Outside My Boat." Both of them will help keep your blood pressure down, because once you step inside an airport anywhere in the world, your life is completely outside your control. You have to immediately take a deep breath, relax, and concentrate on Travel Without Emotion.

You might ask, "Does this always work?" Well, almost always. The exception was a recent trip when I was traveling from La Guardia to Indianapolis with my pregnant wife and two-year-old daughter. Our flight was posted as being delayed an hour and a half. We checked at the counter to make sure the time was correct, they said it was, and off we went to have dinner. After eating a nice, leisurely meal, we returned with twenty minutes to spare before the posted flight time, which was still on the monitors. However, when we got to the gate, there was nobody at the counter.

After looking around we found an airline representative and asked, "What has happened to our flight to Indianapolis?" The answer was, "Oh, that flight has been canceled. I'm sorry you weren't here sooner, because we could have gotten you on another airline to Indianapolis, but now they're completely full."

I must tell you that "Travel Without Emotion" certainly didn't work for me at that moment. In fact, I don't think any acronym would have.

46

Let Go of Stress

TERRY W. DILLMAN

Manager of Worldwide Olympic Marketing, Xerox

WHEN I AWOKE WITH CHEST PAINS that I had never before experienced, I thought, It's got to be some of that spicy Spanish food I had last night. I was too young and in too good physical condition to have that *other* problem, I reassured myself.

I was in Seville, Spain, in late August 1999, attending the World Outdoor Track and Field Championships and supplying USA Track & Field with document-processing equipment for its media operations center.

I got up from my hotel bed, grabbed a glass of water, and attempted to go back to sleep. I did but awoke an hour or so later, sweating, with this elephant sitting on my chest. "I can't believe this is happening," I said to myself. "I'd better check this out."

So at 7 A.M. I got onto the Internet in the Athlete's Hospitality Center and did a search for "angina" and "heart attack." Clearly something was wrong, and it wasn't

158

the food. I met with the U.S. team doctor, Robert Adams, who checked my blood pressure and said, "Call the paramedics. It's better to be safe than sorry. Let's get you to the hospital for a thorough evaluation."

I spent eight hours in a nearby Seville hospital, undergoing tests and speaking English to a hospital staff who only spoke Spanish. The result: no detected heart problems. Two mornings later, the elephant returned, and this time I ventured to one of Seville's top cardiologists. He too could find nothing wrong, but he said to a friend, who translated, "Go home immediately and see your doctor. I don't like what I see on the ECG, but I cannot pinpoint it."

Of course I followed the doctor's orders and arrived in Los Angeles two weeks later. After all, I had to see the rest of the championships and Gehry's Guggenheim in Bilbao, and taste the Michelin three-stars in San Sebastián. I just had to sip some of the reds in Rioja and retrace some old haunts in Barcelona, and I absolutely had to chill out once again on the spectacular beaches on Ibiza.

During this time period something cardiological had definitely happened, although when I wasn't sure. But my Los Angeles cardiologist, during a stress test, said, "You've got some blockage. We're going to have to do an angiogram." And so it was done, as well as an angioplasty with a stent emplacement in the left anterior descending artery, which had been 100 percent blocked.

The growth of corollary arteries, which had taken over from the blocked LADA, had saved my life.

Prior to this experience I had always been somewhat of a Type A personality, mercurial at times, mellow at others, but always willing to have at it whenever something perturbing popped up. My wife had always counseled me to "leave it alone" and "move on." But I was the stubborn type who'd written so many letters to the major airlines that I could have them published as a book (comical and *noir*, no doubt).

No longer. One of the lessons my cardio rehab has taught me—or tried to—is the need to reduce self-induced stress and to "leave it alone." So every day, whether at home or work or commuting, whenever I'm confronted with something I can't control, I tell myself, "Leave it alone. Let it go. It's outside my boat." There's no question it's healthier that way, and sometimes I even follow my own advice.

———————

47

Keep Distracting Thoughts Outside Your Boat

FRANK SHORTER
Olympic gold medalist, marathon, 1972

T HE NIGHT OF THE MASSACRE in Munich during the 1972 Olympic Games, when eleven Israeli athletes were killed by an Arab terrorist group, was very hot and humid. My apartment in the Olympic Village was so crowded that I took my mattress out on the balcony to try to get some rest. I was awakened at about four in the morning by the sounds of gunshots and I couldn't get back to sleep. A few hours later, word spread throughout the Olympic Village that two Israeli athletes had been shot and killed and nine others were being held hostage. All that day, I just stood on my balcony and stared out across the courtyard at the strange man in the ski mask on the other balcony.

The first reaction of most of the athletes was anger. Why me? Why is this happening here? Are they going to postpone the Games? Will my event take place on another day? Will the Olympics be canceled? How can they possibly do this to me? Don't they realize I've been training all my life for this one day?

Most of the athletes then went through the next phase of realizing that regardless of what the sport was, it was not worth the loss of any human lives. Unfortunately, there was still more tragedy to follow at the Munich airport.

After a day's delay and a memorial ceremony, the Games restarted. From that point on, the athletes who were successful were the ones who were able to keep that terrible massacre outside their boat.

Kenny Moore, my U.S. teammate who would finish fourth in the marathon, and I talked at great length about what would happen if the terrorists were to strike again. We felt the worst possible time for an attack would be during the marathon, because it would be absolutely impossible to secure the entire twenty-six-mile course.

I think one of the reasons I won the gold medal in Munich was that I was able to keep all distracting thoughts and fears outside my boat. I concentrated on the fact that I, like all the others, had trained my entire life for this one marathon, this one moment. If the schedule changed, it really didn't make any difference because I still had to go out and run. On the day of the race I never once thought about the possibility of a terrorist attack. I was able to keep that horror outside my boat. Once you let such distractions divert you from your goal, your chance for victory is gone.

**DON'T LET
WHAT YOU CAN'T CONTROL
CONTROL YOU.**

Persistence Pays Off

JACK AGRIOS

Chairman of the board,
Edmonton 2001 World Championships in Athletics

EDMONTON-ALBERTA'S BID for the 2001 World Track and Field Championships actually had its beginnings in 1976, when my two daughters, who were nine and eleven, attended the Olympics in Montreal. We had the opportunity to see all the great athletes compete. Because of this, my daughters became very involved in athletics themselves. A few years later, my oldest daughter happened to be watching the 1993 World Track and Field Championships from Stuttgart on television. She called me and said, "Dad, you've got to come home. You've got to see what's going on in Stuttgart."

I spent the next eight nights with her, watching that wonderful championship, the tremendous competition, the enthusiastic crowd. It was a truly magnificent event. That's when I thought to myself that something like that should come to Edmonton.

The vision and dream of 2001 evolved, and we started our bid process. We quietly went to Athletics Canada without any fanfare, without any publicity, but with the support of the premier and the support of our mayor. Not only were we able to convince Athletics Canada to make a bid for the championships (because it is the federation, it must make the bid) but we also persuaded it that it should support Edmonton-Alberta as the venue. Two months later, following the Atlanta Olympics in 1996, we announced the plans. There was great enthusiasm.

We attended the 1997 championships in Athens with a very small but spirited group of people. Our real concern was that we were competing against bids from Paris, France, and Stanford, California, which had bid two times previously, and Korea, whose bid was going to be chaired by the president of Samsung. Samsung, of course, is one of the largest corporations in the world, and with its financial clout we believed it was definitely the front-runner. Nonetheless, we kept our concerns outside our boat.

Rather than worrying about our competition, we quietly continued our effort to demonstrate why we should succeed. The most important element that existed for us was luck. While our hard work may have helped create our luck, the Asian financial crisis occurred in the fall of 1997. That was not of our making, but as a result the Korean application was no longer viable.

However, once Korea was out of the running, Moscow made a strong potential bid. In September 1998, two months before the winning bid would be decided, the mayor of Moscow made a large financial commitment to bring the championships there. But once again, our good fortune prevailed. While our bid team was in Moscow, the ruble totally devaluated. It went from seven to the U.S. dollar to twenty-two, all in a period of five days. That was totally outside our control, but because of this the bid from Moscow could no longer continue.

When we proceeded to make our bid in November 1998, our remaining opposition was Paris and Stanford. By virtue of our hard work, we were awarded the championships by a 22–2 vote. Everything leading up to that decision was outside our control. Even when faced with what seemed to be insurmountable odds, we didn't give up. We continued our effort and kept our competitors outside our boat. As it turns out, good planning, hard work, and good luck were all instrumental in Edmonton's being awarded the 2001 World Track and Field Championships.

"You can't worry about people who are ahead of you or behind you. Your concentration has to be on what you're doing. Once you lose that concentration, that's when things go awry."

—WALTER PAYTON
NFL Hall of Fame running back

49

Count On Your Work Ethic

TED GIANNOULAS
The Famous Chicken

I WAS HIRED OUT OF COLLEGE by San Diego's KGB radio in 1974. The station offered me two dollars an hour to work dressed up in a chicken suit. It sounded good to me because I just wanted to get my foot in the door. I wasn't looking at dollars, I was looking at the opportunity to get in with a major radio station in town and it appealed to me no matter what the job entailed: shining records, emptying trash cans, or wearing a chicken suit.

I had no experience in theater, no experience in comedy, and no experience in dressing up, not even as a mascot in my own high school. I just applied a strong work ethic to what I was doing, and I didn't give up even though the costume was extremely difficult to wear. I also showed good faith by working overtime without asking for anything in return.

I had no control over my salary or the environment, nor did I have any control as to where I was to go and what I was to do. I simply applied myself fully in the spirit of giving my all. Originally I was supposed to stay for only one week, but the one-week engagement turned into a month and then the month turned into a year. They never told me to stop.

I always believed that new opportunities were bound to arise, and eventually they did. The catalyst for that moment happened four years later, when Ted Turner came to town with the Atlanta Braves and saw what I was doing at the Padres baseball games. He was so impressed he invited me back to perform in Atlanta with the Braves, but he really brought me there to hire me.

He offered me a thousand dollars a week. Just like that. As a matter of fact, I have it on his business card, which I still have to this very day. He called me over in the fourth inning—I was still in my chicken outfit—and had me sit down beside him behind the dugout in Atlanta's Fulton County Stadium. The fans obviously knew what was going on. (It was a sparse crowd because Atlanta was the last-place team in 1978.) He wrote on the back of his business card, "For my pal, Ted Giannoulas, $50,000." He handed it to me and said, "That's our contract. Right there."

Suddenly my life changed. The radio station was on notice that this was serious money. We're talking 1970s dollars. When the radio station offered to match it, Ted doubled his offer. So now I was looking at a six-figure arrangement. Nonetheless, I chose to stay in San Diego, but the fact that there was actually a mini–bidding war over a man in a chicken suit, for crying out loud, brought all kinds of attention. This was incredible to the media. Walter Cronkite talked about it, John Chancellor talked about it, and it was front-page news in San Diego.

On a September night in the fifth inning of a Padres game, right at the height of all the hoopla, I made my announcement that I was staying. The players ran on the field and carried me off on their shoulders like a conquering World Series hero. Ray Kroc, the owner of the Padres at the time, was so appreciative that I would stay and pass on Ted Turner's very generous offer that he threw in $10,000 of his own money on top of what KGB Radio was offering.

But that was really just the beginning. Once again, I didn't see a wage; I saw an opportunity. I made a lot of people very happy with my efforts. I had a feeling, somehow, that the situation would shake out to my benefit. And it did. Eventually different teams approached me and started offering me big money to perform. I went from making minimum wage to being a financial success. Again, all I did was not worry about anything more than what I could control—my work ethic—because that was what was inside my boat.

"Being a single guy in a chicken suit, it's really interesting to see how free-market forces create opportunity for you in so many ways where you least expect it."

—TED GIANNOULAS

"The happiest people I know are the ones who have been able to create a living for themselves around something they truly enjoy doing."

—MICHAEL MCNEAL
Vice president of business development,
PureCarbon, Inc.

50

It's Not What You Are, It's Who You Are

LARRY LINDSTRAND
Four Square Pastor, Assembly of God

WHEN I WAS EIGHTEEN, I was the number one draft choice of the Seattle Mariners. Arizona State, UCLA, Washington State, and Washington were also recruiting me. I had just graduated from Mariner High School in Everett, Washington, where I had been a pitcher and third baseman, with a .653 batting average. I also held the state high school stolen base record. I entered the draft, but I didn't sign a contract because I didn't want to lose my amateur status until I figured out whether I wanted to play pro ball or whether I wanted to go to college.

I planned to take the summer to decide and to go to Europe with two of my buddies. We had already paid for the plane and train tickets to have a last hurrah before we all decided what we were going to do with our lives.

We backpacked across Europe for about two months, and in August we ended up in Paris.

It was a beautiful day. We could see the whole city from the top of the Eiffel Tower. We didn't take the elevator, we thought we'd just run down. Of course, since we were all competitive athletes, we were running down as fast as we could, trying to beat one another.

Three levels from the bottom I slipped, and my foot caught underneath the metal grates. It was kind of a railing where the grate met. I turned the corner, but my foot stayed where it was. My body literally took my knee and twisted it right out of the socket. My foot was looking out the side of my leg. It was incredibly painful. We got a cab to the American hospital. I had completely dislocated the joint, and I had torn all the ligaments and tendons. They reset it as best they could and put me on an airplane. When I got home, my knee was completely reconstructed.

As soon as everybody in baseball found out I had ruined my knee, they just disappeared. The colleges and the pros both deserted me. I went from years of working out with some of the best coaches in our area and developing my skills to three years in rehab trying to get my knee back in shape. Of course, once you hurt your knee like that and you haven't yet proved yourself to the pros, it's all over. I was twenty-one and baseball was now totally outside my boat. I had to let it go.

What got me through was my faith. I had always believed that if you did what you were supposed to do, then everything would work out for the good. If I believed that in the good times, then I should believe that in the bad times, too. I enrolled in a small Christian Bible school, Northwest College in Kirkland, Washington. It was there that I decided my life was going to move in a different direction. I have never regretted that decision.

I'm a pastor now. I've worked the streets of Seattle for years, dealing with many tragic cases. I've discovered that the biggest problem is that people measure their worth by what they do and not by what they have become as a person. Their self-esteem and their identity are based on what they are, not who they are.

When I was in high school, I focused most of my attention not on my athletic abilities, which were God-given gifts, but on me as a person. I concentrated on being accepted for who I was inside my body, rather than being accepted because of my achievements on the baseball or football field. But I temporarily forgot that lesson after my accident. Fortunately, after wallowing around feeling sorry for myself for a couple of weeks, I realized my life had to go on. I could either use my injury as a tool to help me be a better man, husband, and father, or else I could let it eat me up and push me into other things that would destroy my life.

Now I do all my work on the streets. There are a lot of guys out there who have given up. A few years ago I met a doctor sitting on a park bench in Pioneer Square.

The stress had gotten to him, and he had started taking prescription drugs on the side. He'd lost his practice, his wife, his children, and for the last seven years he'd been sitting on skid row living out of cardboard boxes and eating garbage, all because he chose to quit, to give up. I counseled him for about a year. I told him that he could reclaim everything he once had if he would just quit wallowing in self-pity. He had to suck it up and do it. And he did. He got his practice back, his wife back, and his children back, all because he finally stopped identifying who he was as a doctor. He wasn't really a doctor; that was his profession. He was a husband, a father, a man. He finally realized it wasn't what he did that gave him his self-esteem, it was who he was inside.

That's where I've always focused my life: Who am I as a person? What am I going to accomplish? Am I going to use what happened to me for good, or am I going to use it to tear me down and defeat me? I made a choice. I'm going to use it for what I'm good at.

For the last twenty years I've been coaching high school baseball and working with Babe Ruth leagues. Last year I held clinics for our Little League to help kids create skills that will benefit them later on in their lives. In essence, I've never stopped playing. Now I'm living baseball through many youngsters because of the wonderful gift I was given as a high school kid. As a coach my trophies are found in others, and that gives me all the satisfaction I need.

"It's a process every day. What could have been is what could have been. What's important is what's now. I have a choice. Either I can live for now, or I can live in the past, and the past will destroy me."

—LARRY LINDSTRAND

"It's not important what you used to be. No one will remember what you used to be. What difference are you making today? That's what's important."

—LARRY LINDSTRAND

"You wake up today, you enjoy today. You have no control of tomorrow and you've lost control of yesterday. You go inning by inning."

—JOE TORRE
Manager, New York Yankees

**SOMETIMES WE SAIL
WITH THE WIND;
SOMETIMES WE SAIL
AGAINST THE WIND.**

51

Have Faith in Your Shipmates

PETER ISLER

Sailboat skipper, commentator, author

IN MY EVOLUTION as a competitive sailboat racer, I have learned to concern myself only with the things that are in my ability to change. In the early days when I started skippering and some sort of snafu occurred, such as when a sail got ripped or there was some delay in bringing a sail down, I'd try to manage. Even though I was at the very back of the boat, as far away from the problem as someone could be and still be on the boat, I'd start screaming and yelling and telling my shipmates what I thought they should do. I'd be completely involved verbally with the efforts to rectify the problem.

As I matured as a sailboat racer, I noticed myself screaming and yelling and getting verbally involved less and less when things went wrong, which they always do. You can't control them. They're outside your boat.

Now I'm just quiet back there, sailing away and worrying about what I should worry about, which is how to keep the boat going as fast as possible in the best possible direction.

I realized that all my screaming and yelling wasn't helping at all. I was just adding to the cacophony and the mayhem that was already going on. In the end, I learned you really have to trust your crew. There's a bunch of good people up there who are hands-on and dealing with the problem, and it's very rare when somebody in the back of the boat is going to be able to help them by providing some sort of insight they can't see from right up close.

It reminds me of Dennis Conner versus Ted Turner; when something goes wrong on the boat when Dennis is on board in an America's Cup race, he's completely quiet. You hear no screaming or yelling. Dennis is amazingly calm. I learned from him that it doesn't help to get involved when you're the helmsman of the boat. You do your job and let the other guys do their jobs.

On the other hand, Ted Turner is more of a screamer and a yeller. That's just his personality. Sometimes it limits him a little bit in terms of how his crew handles situations. But usually when he gets involved he's more apt to shout encouragement than to shout the obvious, such as, "Get that broken sail down out of the rig!" That doesn't help. Ted is more of the cajoling type, with words like, "Come on guys, I love you, work hard, get it, get it done. We need that sail, guys, go, go!"

———————————

"We didn't design the seas, so we can't control the currents; and we didn't design the boat, so we can't make it impregnable; but we can steer to our own satisfaction and let go of the rest."

—DR. JOYCE BROTHERS
Psychologist, author, and speaker

52

Sail Your Own Boat

JJ ISLER

Olympic silver and bronze medalist in sailing;
four-time Rolex Yachtswoman of the Year

IN SAILING, THERE'S A BALANCE of how much you worry about your competitors and how much you sail your own race. In the last race in the women's 470 class in the 2000 Sydney Olympics, there were four teams that were mathematically tied for second: the United States, the Ukrainians, the Israelis, and the Germans. The Australians had eight points on the field, so they most likely had the gold medal wrapped up unless they sank.

Partway through the race, I realized I was spending way too much time worrying about where the Israelis were, where the Germans were, and what the Ukrainians were doing. It's tempting to get distracted and make it a game of counting the boats between you and each mark. I realized whatever happened in this race was going to happen and I should just relax and enjoy it. At that point we were in fourth place overall and my counting little boats wasn't going to make them go away.

We decided to change our focus and worry about our own boat, and just look for the wind coming to us. On the last run we sailed to the edge of the course, where we thought there would be some current relief and some acceleration of wind around the point. We got there, and the next thing we knew, we'd passed a whole clump of boats and gone from fourth overall to second, thus clinching the silver medal for the United States.

Once I freed my mind to spend more time looking at the patterns we were seeing in the wind instead of worrying about the other guys, I could think about where we were going. It allowed us to anticipate what we were going to do next, instead of reacting to where the other boats were.

"The Olympics is bigger than anything. And the logistical hassles are really outside of your control. You can't micromanage them. At the Olympic level the athletes who are able to make it are the ones who don't get flustered by all those little things that can really frazzle you."

—JJ ISLER

"It's amazing how many people come up to you and say, 'Are you ready to win?' That's outside of my boat. I'm ready to perform my best inside my boat, and that's all you can ask of me."

—JJ ISLER

**EVERY SO OFTEN
YOU HAVE TO
TACK AWAY FROM
THE FLEET TO FIND
THE BEST WIND.**

53

You Can Control How You React to Others' Decisions

REGGIE RIVERS

Radio talk-show host; college football television analyst; author; former NFL player, Denver Broncos

As an NFL rookie free agent in 1991, I didn't think I was going to make the Denver Broncos, but I did. The next year I made the team again and became the starting fullback. I was playing really well, and things were going great. I've always had confidence that if I get an opportunity I'll do my best, and if my best is good enough for me to be the starter, that's great. If my best is not good enough, then I'll move on and I'll do something else.

After my second year, we had a coaching change. Dan Reeves left, and Wade Phillips came in. He brought with him a whole new coaching staff and a bunch of free-agents to whom they were paying a lot of money, including two running backs, Rod Bernstine and Robert Delpino. Rod Bernstine was going to be the new tail-back, and Robert Delpino was supposed to be the new fullback. Well, I was the incumbent starting fullback, and I thought, You know what, I can't control who they bring in here, but I can control how I'm going to perform in training camp. I had it in my head that I was not going to get beaten out by this guy.

We went to minicamps, and when they ended I was still the starting fullback. We went to training camp, and through the first four weeks, I was still the starting fullback. We were learning a new offense, and whenever I'm learning something new I feel I have an advantage, because I have good study habits. I had the best camp of my career, I didn't drop a pass, I didn't have a fumble, I didn't have a missed assignment. I was playing so much better than Robert Delpino that they couldn't replace me with him.

When the season began, I was the starting fullback. Although Delpino was making four times as much money as I was, he was sitting on the bench. Three games into the season was our bye week. The running backs coach called me in and said, "You know what, Reggie, it's nothing you've done wrong, but we brought Delpino here to be the starter, so we're going to make him the starter."

I went home, and I was really mad. I couldn't control what decision they made, but I always had confidence that if I played well and I was the one who deserved to start, I would. For the next three weeks all I could do was brood about this. I was upset. I wasn't working very hard in practice, I wasn't working very hard on special teams, I had a bad attitude about everything. I sat in the back of the meeting rooms and thought everything was fruitless. It didn't matter what I did, they were going to make some other decision. I just felt like the situation was hopeless.

Luckily for me, our special teams coach, Richard Smith, pulled me aside one day and said, "Reggie, you've got a decision to make. Now, I know you feel like you got screwed because they took the starting job away from you. But you're still in the NFL, you're still on this football team, and you've got an opportunity to make plays on special teams. You're still the backup fullback. You might get another opportunity, but if you keep going the way you're going, you'll be cut in the next couple of weeks because you're just not performing."

I went home and really thought about that. I weighed the whole situation. I returned the next day with my mind made up. I was just going to focus on what I could control, not on the outside situation. What I could control was what I did in meetings every day, what I did in the weight room, what I did in practice, and how I performed with the opportunities that were given to me. I ended up having the best season of my NFL career. On special teams I became completely unblockable on kickoff coverage. I must have made a third of our tackles on kickoff coverage, and I went to the Pro Bowl.

I look back and think that was the one time in my life where I got outside of myself. I got out of the mentality of hey, I'm just going to control what I can control, and instead I started to get frustrated by decisions that other people were making. But once I let go of that and put it outside my boat and said, "Okay, I'll get back to controlling what I can control," I ended up having the best year of my career.

————————

"Being gifted intellectually is only a small part of the equation of success. Concentrate on the factors you have control over: persistence, self-discipline, confidence. Far more failures are due to lack of will than lack of ability."

—TERRY BRADSHAW
NFL Hall of Fame quarterback; sports broadcaster

54

Keep Prejudice Outside Your Boat

RON MIX

Attorney; NFL Hall of Fame offensive tackle,
San Diego Chargers

A THLETICS TO ME HAS ALWAYS represented something very special that goes beyond exercise and entertainment. Athletics is an activity that helps foster some of our fundamental values, such as loyalty, respect for authority, discipline, hard work, and, more than anything, judging a person as an individual.

The best example I can think of took place when I was playing with the Chargers in the mid-1960s and we were on an eastern road swing. In those days, a road swing meant just that: we stayed back east for three weeks. We set up camp at Niagara Falls, on the U.S. side of the border, and we would train at a high school on the Canadian side of the border. We would play the New York Jets, return and train for a week at Niagara Falls,

189

then play the Boston Patriots, return and train, and then play the Buffalo Bills.

We'd go to practice in two buses, the coaches in a Volkswagen bus and the players in a regular-size bus. For some reason, on this particular day the coaches' bus had been delayed at the border and the players' bus arrived at the high school field on a typically brutal Canadian winter day with the temperature about 15 degrees F. and the windchill factor well below zero.

We waited fifteen minutes, and no coaches arrived. Twenty minutes, and still no coaches. Finally, our quarterback, John Hadl, said, "Well, we've got to do something to keep warm." Halfback Paul Lowe chimed in, "Let's play a game of touch football." Lance Alworth added, "Yeah, let's play offense against the defense," and then Ernie Ladd, our 6'9", 340-pound tackle, said, "No, let's play the blacks against the whites." All the black guys started laughing, running to the other side of the field. They wouldn't let me play because I'm Jewish, so they made me the referee.

What was striking to me about the whole thing was that here was a group of men from every social, economic, racial, and religious background you can imagine, and we'd come together for a common purpose. We lived together and played together and did things together, and what we learned was that people are basically the same. They have the same dreams and aspirations and the same desire to make life better for their families than it was for them. That's what athletics teaches.

It's interesting that we had grown so comfortable with one another that we could joke about such ridiculous notions as the artificial separation of people by race or religion, and this was at a time when the civil rights movement was barely getting started. Yet look at the human lessons we had learned.

We learned that if we can keep all of those preconceived ideas about people, all different kinds of people, outside our boat, then we open ourselves to getting to know them inside our boat.

I first learned this lesson when I was attending the University of Southern California. That was a time when Jews and African Americans could not join fraternities and football teams were made up primarily of Protestant, white Anglo-Saxons. Yet at the same time, Willie Wood, later Hall of Fame safety for the Green Bay Packers, an African American, and I, a Jew, were elected cocaptains of the USC football team. Our teammates thought we had the right stuff leaders are supposed to have.

This is another example of how athletics provides an environment where people are judged as individuals. As far as our teammates were concerned, being African American or being Jewish was outside their boat. They were interested only in who could best lead them to the Rose Bowl. That's what mattered inside their boat.

"I don't think leadership is giving people direction. Leadership is giving people something they believe in that they're willing to risk their life to accomplish. They don't care how tough it is because they know they can do it. Your job is to convince them of that and then get out of their way so they don't run over you."

—ED HUBBARD
U.S. Air Force colonel, retired

55

Recognize Reality

ART NOEHREN
Golf course architect

I HAVE A VERY STRONG FEELING that we as human beings have very little control over our lives. We're all conditioned by our past and our upbringing. We're conditioned to respond in a certain way on what's good and what's bad, what we like and what we don't like.

Many of our responses are subconscious. We act in a way we think is free, but we're really not free. We think we are intelligent, rational people who can decide our own fate, yet to a very large degree we can't. We're sort of thrown into the winds because of the way our memories work. Our memories are very catchy; they cling to things that make us successful. It's programming. It's outside our boat.

Once we recognize that we are a certain way, that's a major step. Then, when you see your life going along, you can say, "I'm reacting this way because that's who I am." When your business partner acts a certain way, you

193

can say, "She's just being who she is." This awareness makes you more forgiving of yourself and of the people around you.

"At the end of the day we tend to go back to our roots. The wonder of the world is that there are patterns, and if you look long enough and think hard enough and discover them, it can make a dramatic difference in how you do business."

–DOUG HALL
Author of *Jump Start Your Business Brain*

"You win some and you lose some—but you just need to say, 'That's outside my boat.' "

–LAMAR HUNT
Owner, NFL Kansas City Chiefs

THE 80 PERCENT OF YOUR LIFE THAT DOESN'T COUNT IS OUTSIDE YOUR BOAT. DON'T LET IT INSIDE YOUR BOAT, WHERE IT CAN REALLY MESS UP THE 20 PERCENT THAT DOES COUNT.

Contributors

BE UNSINKABLE.

Made in the USA
Columbia, SC
07 August 2022